ROCK*
UPGRADE

Thank you for purchasing the print edition of **Building WordPress Themes from Scratch**! For a complimentary copy of the book in **pdf**, **mobi**, and **epub** format, please forward your Amazon receipt via email to: *upgrade@rockablepress.com*

ROCKABLE*

Rockablepress.com
Envato.com

© Rockable Press 2012

All rights reserved. No part of this publication may be reproduced or redistributed in any form without the prior written permission of the publishers.

Dedication

To my parents, Louis and Marie; I wouldn't be who I am without you. Thank you for encouraging and supporting me, even though I could be a pain in the neck sometimes.

Table of Contents

Contents

Dedication 2

Introduction 7

Why I Wrote This 7
Who is this Book for? 7
What this Book Includes 8
WordPress Basics 8
   Posts 9
   Pages 9
   Menus 10
Coding Conventions 11
Plan of Action 12

Converting HTML to a WordPress Theme 15

Building Our HTML Theme 15
   Files & Structure 16
   Markup & CSS 16
style.css/CSS 20
Functions.php 22
Theme Template Hierarchy 26
Header & Footer 28
The Loop 37
The Post Pages 39
   The Index 39
   Single Page Template 44
   Content Pages 47
Auxiliary Template Pages 49
   The Sidebar Template 49
   Archives Template 52
   The 404 Error Template 54
Building Our Own Framework 56
   Principles of Reuse 56

Table of Contents

Define Your Needs — 57
Existing Theme Frameworks — 59
Coding Tips for Frameworks/Child Themes — 60

Creating Custom Post Types — 63

Designing the Custom Post Type — 63
Building it into the Theme — 65
Setting up the Custom Post Type — 65
Modifying the Businesses Admin Panel — 77
Listing Custom Post Types — 80
Creating a Custom Post Type Single Template — 85
Creating the Homepage — 90
Querying Posts — 91

Creating a Theme Options Page — 101

Creating the Admin Page — 101
Adding Settings to the Template — 109
OptionTree Plugin by Envato — 112
Creating Widgets — 113

Plugin Development — 123

Defining the Plugin — 123
The Shortcode — 127
The Template Tag — 130

Resources — 133

Theme & Plugin Directories — 133
Coding Resources — 137
Final Thoughts — 139
Stay Up to Date! — 140

About The Author — 142

Your Download Links — 143

INTRODUCTION

Introduction

When I first got into web development, all the way back in 2002, a tool like WordPress did not exist yet. As a matter of fact, it wouldn't be until almost a year later that WordPress would be released to the public for the first time; not that I was ready to use WordPress at initial release. I actually didn't start using it until 2004 (around WordPress 1.5), when my friend told me about this new blogging platform that I should consider instead of writing my own.

I instantly fell in love, hacking away, learning the platform, making my own changes (sometimes to the core[1]), and watching it grow over the years. What started out as a simple, open source blogging platform is now a super-powerful content management system (CMS) that can boast that it's the most widely-used CMS on the Internet.[2] In this book, I plan to teach you how to use WordPress, as well as how to leverage the API to create your own custom themes, plugins, and content types. In other words, I will show you how to make WordPress your own.

Why I Wrote This

WordPress is living platform with constant updates and major enhancements released every 6-12 months. At the time of this writing, WordPress 3.3 had just been released with quite a few new, really nice features. Because of this ever-changing landscape, it's important to keep users updated on the latest and greatest WordPress capabilities.

Who is this Book for?

I'd like to say that this book is for anyone interested in WordPress, regardless of background. However, to keep it streamlined, I do make some assumptions about you, dear reader. I assume that you

---

[1] This is really, really not recommended.

[2] http://trends.builtwith.com/cms

have a solid understanding of HTML, CSS, Javascript, PHP and MySQL. I also assume that you've at least looked at the WordPress Codex, which can be found at codex.wordpress.org. I will be looking at converting HTML to a WordPress theme, building plugins, and more, all from scratch. So, if you've never done that, this book should be right up your alley. I do assume you have programmed before, however, which brings us to...

What this Book Includes

Packaged with this book, you will find:

1. A set of PSD files for the Homepage, Directory Page, Blog, and Single Business Page.

2. A set of HTML files created from the PSDs. They will be used to create the Director WordPress theme. On top of the four pages created from the PSDs, the HTML folder includes a */css/* folder for four CSS files: `style.css`, `reset.css`, `master.css`, and `ie.css`. All images used in the HTML template are also included.

3. A fully functioning WordPress theme called Director. This can be found in the */director/* folder.

These files and themes may be used freely in your projects, both commercial and non-commercial. However, they may not be redistributed or resold in any way. As you work through this book you may choose to either construct your own set of files from scratch, or use the example files as a guide. The link to download these files is at the end of the book.

WordPress Basics

In this book, I assume you have at least used WordPress as a blogging platform or CMS. Because of that, during each section I will not explain how to create a post, a page, or a menu item. I will offer

Introduction

9

some quick how-tos here. If you'd like to read more, the WordPress Codex has a great "Getting Started" site.[2b]

Posts

Here are the basics for creating a post in WordPress. It's in the *Posts* section that you will add blog posts, news articles, and anything else that gets updated regularly. This is also how you will create custom post types. Just replace "Posts" in the first step with the menu name of the Post Types (you will read more on that later).

- Click the *Posts* tab.

- Click the *Add New* sub-tab.

- Start filling in the blanks: title, body text, etc.

- As needed, select a category, add tags, and make other selections from the sections below and to the right of the post.

- When you are ready, click *Publish.*

- To view a post, click the *View Post* button beneath the post title.

Pages

Adding and editing pages are essentially the same as adding and editing posts.

- Click the *Pages* tab.

- Click the *Add New* sub-tab.

- Start filling in the blanks: title, body text, etc.

- Select the parent, template, and order as needed.

- When you are ready, click *Publish.*

[2b] http://codex.wordpress.org/Getting_Started_with_WordPress

10 Introduction

- To view a page, click the *View Page* button beneath the page title.

Menus

Since WordPress 3.0, WordPress has added the ability to create and manage navigation menus from right within WordPress.

To create new menus:

1. Go to *Appearance* ➤ *Menus.*

2. Create a new menu by pressing the "+" tab.

3. Fill out the menu name and press *Create Menu*.

4. You can then add custom links, pages, categories, and custom post types by checking off the corresponding items on the left and clicking *Add to Menu*.

5. You can reorder the menu items by dragging and dropping them. If you want to create a sub- or drop-down menu, select the menu item, place it underneath the item you want to be the parent, and drag it slightly to the right.

6. Once your menu is complete, press *Save Menu*.

7. If your theme supports multiple menus, you may need to associate your new menu with a "theme location." You can do so using the drop down box on the left, under the *Theme Locations* heading. We will see how these work later in the book.

WordPress has its own extensive documentation on creating menus in the codex.[2c]

[2c] http://codex.wordpress.org/Appearance_Menus_SubPanel#Create_a_Menu

Introduction   **11**

Coding Conventions

I plan on using the best practices that I know, including the ones laid out in the WordPress Codex.[3] This means that I will do my best to write correct markup, name variables properly, create constants when necessary, and include thorough, clear comments within all of my programming.

I will also take on the following convention for printing code as used in previous WordPress books published by Rockable. This means that all lines of code will appear against a light grey background in a fixed-width typeface, like this:

```
<?php echo 'Hello World!'; ?>
```

Sometimes a line of code is too long to fit entirely on one line. In this case, the grey background of the following line (or lines, for a **really** long line) will be slightly indented. In most cases, a space character is permissable between the last character on the initial line and the first character on the next line. If a space is **not** allowed, there will be a continuation marker (▶) to remind you. For example, here a space is permitted between "**dog.'** " and "**?>**":

```
<?php echo 'The quick brown fox jumped over the lazy dog.'
    ?>
```

But in the following code, there is **no** space intended after the underscore. Therefore "**pingback_url**" is correct:

```
<link rel="pingback" href="<?php bloginfo('pingback_    ▶
    url'); ?>" />
```

Note: when copy-pasting the code out of the book, you'll need to take out these arrows and accompanying space. With this in mind, let's take a look at the plan of action for the rest of this book.

---

[3] http://codex.wordpress.org/WordPress_Coding_Standards

Plan of Action

This book should read much like a long, multi-part tutorial. I want to take you through my design process, explaining what I do (and why I do it) on every step of the way. Here's what I'll be doing:

- **Converting HTML/CSS to a Dynamic WordPress Theme** – I've been provided with a PSD (included with the book) that I've transformed into HTML. The first part of this book will be taking the resulting HTML/CSS and converting it to a WordPress theme. Along the way, I'll talk about the various theme pages we're working with, the WordPress theme hierarchy, and of course, the WordPress Loop.

- **Creating a Custom Post Type** – This, in my humble opinion, is one of the best additions to WordPress in recent releases. With the ability to make your own content types — each with its own theme template — you can take WordPress from being a CMS limited to blog posts and pages, to a CMS that can manage any kind of content you can imagine. In this book, we'll be creating a business listing type, which will allow us to create a business directory.

- **Theme Options and Widgets** – With WordPress, you can make a theme your own by adding a theme options page and custom widgets. In these sections, we'll make it very easy for people who use our themes to add their own customizations without delving into the code or creating a child theme.

- **Creating a Plugin** – One of the most powerful facets of WordPress is the fact that it's pluggable. We can add functionality to our installation of WordPress without changing the core WordPress files. There are vast directories of free[4] and premium[5] plugins that vastly expand the capabilities of

---

[4] http://wordpress.org/extend/plugins/
[5] http://codecanyon.net/category/plugins/wordpress

Introduction   **13**

WordPress. In the final section of this book, we will build our own plugin.

This book should serve as a very linear guide to WordPress development. That being said, my hope is that you can visit any chapter of the book (or at least any of the four sections I've laid out) for quick reference. So without further ado, let's get started!

Converting HTML to a WordPress Theme

Converting HTML to a WordPress Theme

Building Our HTML Theme

Included with this book are a few things: the Photoshop files (PSDs) from which the design came, the HTML templates I created from the PSDs, and the fully functional WordPress theme. While we won't be going over slicing and dicing the PSDs, I will take this opportunity to explain the HTML template to an extent, because I want you to be somewhat familiar with the basis for our WordPress theme. Going forward, keep in mind that we're building a business directory website. Here is a screenshot of what the design will look like:

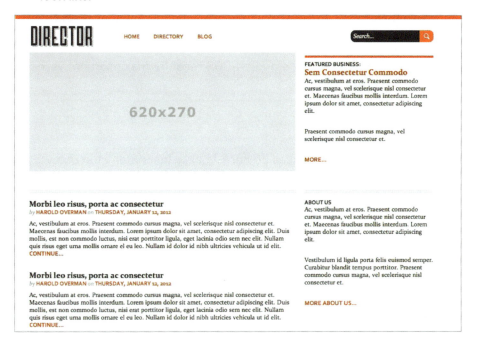

16   **Converting HTML to a WordPress Theme**

Files & Structure

You will find four HTML files we're going to convert (one for each PSD):

- `index.html` – The homepage design
- `blog.html` – A blog post listing page
- `directory.html` – A business listing page
- `business.html` – A single business page

All of our themes pages will be derived from the markup on these pages.

You will also find two folders: an *images* folder, where all theme images will go (there are not many), and a *css* folder, where all of the CSS will go. Within the *css* folder, there are four CSS files that make up a simple framework I use for styling my websites (thank you, Dan Cederholm). They are:

- `reset.css` – Your standard CSS reset for maximum browser compatibility.
- `master.css` – The crux of the matter. All of the main CSS lives here.
- `ie.css` – Any IE fixes go here. Luckily there aren't too many.
- `style.css` – This will simply import the other three style-sheets (in the order I've listed them here. That is **very** important).

You will also find a *img* folder within the *css* folder. Any images that are called within the CSS go in this folder.

Markup & CSS

If you take a look at one of the HTML files, I think you will see some pretty standard markup. I am using HTML5, which requires a few lines of code to make it work.

Converting HTML to a WordPress Theme

17

The first line is the doctype declaration, which is simply:

```
<!DOCTYPE html>
```

Once HTML5 sees adoption from all browsers and older browsers are phased out, this is all that will be necessary in order to use it. However, right now we do have older browsers that do not support it (I'm looking at you, IE), so we need some JavaScript magic in order to make it work. We will be using the invaluable html5shiv,[6] which will add HTML5 elements to the Document Object Model (DOM), so that we can add style definitions for them in our CSS, and if we so desire, we can manipulate them using JavaScript. The line is simply:

```
<!--[if lt IE 9]> <script src="http://html5shim.googlecode.
com/svn/trunk/html5.js"></script> <![endif]-->
```

In plain English, this is saying, "If the browser is IE8 or lower, call this JavaScript." That's all we need; we can now use HTML5 as we please!

The CSS (most of which is in `master.css`) is also pretty self-explanatory. I will point out that I tried to use percentages for widths whenever I could, giving us a more flexible grid to work with. There is a big trend toward "responsive web design," which aims to make a website device agnostic.[7] While that is outside the scope of this book (not that I'm an expert), flexible grids help us considerably with designing flexible, responsive websites.

In order to achieve this flexibility, I created a class called `#container` with the following definition:

```
#container {
    margin: 0 auto;
    text-align: left;
    width: 70%; /* Target: 940px; */
```

---

[6] http://code.google.com/p/html5shim/

[7] http://www.abookapart.com/products/responsive-web-design

18 Converting HTML to a WordPress Theme

```
    padding: 10px 0;
}
```

This will ensure that our entire layout takes up 70% of the browser window and centers the content. The comment tells the reader that from here on out, I will base my widths on a 940px wide layout. In reality, the layout will expand and contract with the size of the browser window.[8]

I also have a few general CSS classes I use throughout the template. Since this is a 2-column layout, I created classes for both the left and right columns:

```
.left-col {
    width: 66%;
    float: left;
}

.right-col {
    float: right;
    width: 32%;
    margin-left: 2%;
}
```

As you can see, .left-col (for left column — I'm very clever) will take up 66% of #container and float to the left. Conversely, .right-col (for... well, I think you've got it) will take up 32% of #container, floating right. This leaves 2% wiggle[9] room, which I used for a margin to separate the two columns. I also have two separate but similar CSS classes to easily float individual elements left or right:

```
.left {
    float: left;
}
```

---

[8] For more on flexible grids, Ethan Marcotte has an excellent article: http://www.alistapart.com/articles/fluidgrids/

[9] ... wiggle, wiggle, wiggle, wiggle. Yeah.

Converting HTML to a WordPress Theme

19

```css
.right {
    float: right;
}
```

These classes are also aptly named. To ensure none of these four classes extend past where they should and end up eating the rest of the page, I employ a nice little hack that Dan Cederholm came up with for self-clearing floats:

```css
.group:after {
    content: ".";
    display: block;
    height: 0;
    clear: both;
    visibility: hidden;
}
```

Now, for any containing `div` that has floating elements, we can also apply the class name **group** and everything will stay within the container:

```html
<div id="main" class="group">
    <div class="left">One Fish</div>
    <div class="right">Two Fish</div>
</div>
```

There is a fix we need to apply to make it work in IE 6 and 7, which you can find in the `ie.css` file:

```css
* html .group { /* IE6 */
    height: 1%;
}

*:first-child+html .group { /* IE7 */
    min-height: 1px;
}
```

To read more about self-clearing floats (and better CSS in general), I strongly recommend *Handcrafted CSS* by Dan Cederholm.[10]

[10] http://handcraftedcss.com/

20 Converting HTML to a WordPress Theme

I'll explain any other markup or CSS along the way. Right now, let's get in to actually building the theme! We'll start by creating our theme folder — let's call it /director/[11] and copying the /css/ folder into it.

style.css/CSS

Whenever I convert an HTML template to a WordPress theme, I start first with `style.css`, since it's the easiest file to convert (plus, it defines the theme in WordPress). What I do is remove `style.css` from the /css/ directory and move it into the root theme directory (in this case /director/). At this point, our file structure looks like this:

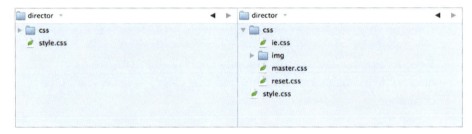

Now, we're going to modify `style.css` a bit. Open it up in your favorite text editor, and start by adding the theme definition at the very top, starting at line 1:

```
/*
Theme Name:   Director
Theme URI:    http://www.envato.com
Description:  A business directory theme.
Version:      1.0
Author:       Joe Casabona
Author URI:   http://www.casabona.org
*/
```

This gives WordPress everything it needs to know to list our theme in the *Themes* ➤ *Appearance* section of our WordPress installation.

[11] Later on we'll be uploading this to *wp-contents/themes/*

Converting HTML to a WordPress Theme 21

There is one more thing we need to do to this file, and that's adjust the references to the other stylesheets. Since we moved `style.css` up one directory, we'll need to change each import to include "`css/`" like so:

```
@import url("css/reset.css");
@import url("css/master.css");
@import url("css/ie.css");
```

Much better! Our CSS is now all set up and ready to use. Before we move on though, I want to add some CSS to `css/master.css` to account for WordPress's default classes to position images through the editor. So let's open up `master.css` and add this code:

```
img.centered, .aligncenter, div.aligncenter {
    display: block;
    margin-left: auto;
    margin-right: auto;
}

.alignright {
    float: right;
}

.alignleft {
    float: left;
}
```

This will ensure that when a user positions an image using the WordPress editor, the image will behave properly.[12] Next, let's add some default styles to be used when the user adds a caption:

```
.wp-caption {
    border: 1px solid #ddd;
    text-align: center;
    background-color: #d4d4d4;
    padding-top: 4px;
```

---

[12] We can actually consolidate `.left` and `.alignleft`, and `.right` and `.alignright`. I left them separate for illustration purposes.

22   Converting HTML to a WordPress Theme

```css
    margin: 10px;
}

.wp-caption img {
  margin: 0;
  padding: 0;
  border: 0 none;
}

.wp-caption p.wp-caption-text {
  font-size: 0.85em;
  line-height: 1.214em;
  padding: 0 4px 5px;
  margin: 0;
}
```

Perfect! With that taken care of, let's move on to the second half of our theme prep-work, which is creating the `functions.php` file.

Functions.php

The `functions.php` file is where you make your theme magic happen. It's worth noting that you do not need this particular file, but according to the WordPress codex:

> **❝** This file basically acts like a plugin, and if it is present in the theme you are using, it is automatically loaded during WordPress initialization (both for admin pages and external pages). **❞**[13]

You can add features like sidebars, navigation menus, thumbnail support, and more. We'll also employ the help of our `functions.php` file later on to declare our custom post type, but for now, we're just going to:

- Define two constants that we'll use in our theme.

---

[13] http://codex.wordpress.org/Theme_Development#Functions_File

Converting HTML to a WordPress Theme

23

- Add menu support.

- Add support for a sidebar.

So in the *director/* folder, create a `functions.php` file and add the following lines:

```php
<?php
define( 'TEMPPATH', get_bloginfo('stylesheet_directory'));
define( 'IMAGES', TEMPPATH. "/images");
?>
```

What we're doing here is creating two constants. `TEMPPATH` will be the path to our theme's directory. This will make it easier to link to any extra files we might want to include, such as other stylesheets, JavaScript, and more. We do this using the `get_bloginfo()` function.

The functions `get_bloginfo()` and `bloginfo()`[14] are incredibly useful functions that pull all kinds of general information about the WordPress installation. Besides the site name, it will grab the description (or tagline), the RSS URL, the full theme path, the home/blog URL, the admin email, and more.[15] We will be using `bloginfo()` quite a bit as we move forward.

`IMAGES` uses `TEMPPATH` and appends our images folder to it, so that we'll have an easier time linking to any theme specific images. Speaking of the *images/* folder, why don't we go ahead and add that to the *director/* theme.

Next, we'll add menu support so that the theme user will be able to change the navigation without having to rely on a developer or having to know how to write their own code. Before the closing PHP tag (`?>`), add in this code:

```php
add_theme_support('nav-menus');
if ( function_exists('register_nav_menus')) {
```

[14] `bloginfo()` prints the value, `get_bloginfo()` returns it.

[15] Read all about it here: http://codex.wordpress.org/Function_Reference/bloginfo

```
register_nav_menus(
    array(
        'main' => 'Main Nav'
    )
);
}
```

There are a couple things going on here. First, we're using Word-Press's built-in function, `add_theme_support()`, to tell WordPress that we want to be able to have dynamic nav menus. Then, after making sure the function is defined,[16] we call `register_nav_menus()`, sending it an array of menus that we'd like to create as key => value pairs, where the key is the slug and the value is the display name. In this case, we are only sending one key => value pair, because we only need one menu, but we could send several if the theme called for it.

Our last step (for now) is to add in sidebar support for our theme. Just like with the menu, we'll make sure the proper function (in this case, `register_sidebar`) works, then we'll call it to create the sidebar:

```
if ( function_exists( 'register_sidebar' ) ) {
    register_sidebar( array (
        'name' => __( 'Primary Sidebar', 'primary-sidebar' ),
        'id' => 'primary-widget-area',
        'description' => __( 'The primary widget area', 'dir' ),
        'before_widget' => '<div class="widget">',
        'after_widget' => "</div>",
        'before_title' => '<h3 class="widget-title">',
        'after_title' => '</h3>',
    ) );
}
```

---

[16] We should code our theme to work properly with current and older WordPress installations.

Converting HTML to a WordPress Theme

With `register_sidebar()`,[17] we're creating a highly customizable sidebar based on a list of arguments sent as an array. We're assigning the sidebar a name, ID, and description, and then we're telling WordPress the markup for each section (or widget). The last four arguments can list any HTML markup, and WordPress will print it appropriately, but if you look at our HTML template, you'll see this markup matches our template perfectly. The arguments `before_widget` and `after_widget` list the markup that the widget will be wrapped in, and `before_title` and `after_title` list the markup that the widget's title will be wrapped in. So this:

… will be displayed using this markup, as defined in our functions file:

```
<div class="widget">
    <h3 class="widget-title">Hello World!</h3>
    <p>Here is some content for a widget!</p>
</div>
```

Later, we'll define our entire sidebar using the sidebar template.

That's everything we'll need for our `functions.php` file at this point, but we will come back to it, I promise! Right now, let's get into the good stuff; we will actually convert our HTML template into a working WordPress theme.

---

[17] Codex link: http://codex.wordpress.org/Function_Reference/register_sidebar

Theme Template Hierarchy

When deciding how to display content to the user, WordPress relies on a very sophisticated template hierarchy based on the theme's template names. The only pages that are actually required to make a theme work properly are `style.css`, which has the theme definition in it, and `index.php`, which is the template that's used if WordPress cannot find any other template files. In addition to these two essential template files, we can also design different templates for pages, single posts, category pages, tags, taxonomies, and more. For even more control, we can get specific with pages, tags, categories, and post-types. For example, if we had a custom post type named "movies," we could create a template named `single-movies.php`, which would automatically be used to display posts of that type. Of course, we don't **need** a `single-movies.php` template. The drill down in WordPress would look like this:

1. `single-movies.php`

2. `single.php`

3. `index.php`

We have similar templates drilling down for categories, pages, tags, etc. We can also create page templates that we can apply to specific pages. The convention (though this is not a requirement) is to give the template's PHP file a name that semantically describes it. For example, if we wanted a one-column page template, we could name it **page-one-column.php**. The only extra code we'd need to add is a comment at the beginning of the template that looks like this:

```
/*
Template Name: One Column
*/
```

Converting HTML to a WordPress Theme

This PHP comment will tell WordPress to offer the "One Column" page as a template in the WordPress editor:

This template will supersede any other page-specific template that can be applied to the page. For example, if our page ID is 13, and we have a `page-13.php` template, the One Column template will override the `page-13.php` template. Similar to our single templates, there WordPress applies a hierarchy (or drill down) to pages, applying them in this order of preference:

1. A specific page template (like `page-one-column.php`) that was chosen within the WordPress editor
2. `page-<slug>.php`. If our page's slug[18] is "about-us," the template name would be `page-about-us.php`
3. `page-<id>.php`
4. `page.php`
5. `index.php`

Finally, WordPress accounts for certain non-content specific sections of the theme by assigning them their own templates. These sections include, but are not limited to:[19]

[18] A URL-friendly version of the page name.
[19] I've included the template name, a description, and the WordPress function used to call that template.

28   **Converting HTML to a WordPress Theme**

- `header.php` – Anything above the content area. This will likely include the HTML, head, and beginning body tags, as well as possibly the site name, searchbar, and navigation. Function call: `get_header()`

- `footer.php` – Anything below the content area. This will close out the body and HTML tags, and it will also (appropriately) include the site footer. Function call: `get_footer()`

- `sidebar.php` – This determines the site's sidebar. There can also be multiple implementations of the sidebar by creating `sidebar-<name>.php`. So if we want a different sidebar for the "About" page, we can create `sidebar-about.php`. Function call: `get_sidebar()` or `get_sidebar('about')`

- `searchform.php` – This will customize the display of the search bar. Function call: `get_search_form()`

The WordPress Codex[20] has extensive documentation on the template hierarchy here: http://codex.wordpress.org/Template_Hierarchy, which includes a handy flow chart (see following page 29).

Let's start our conversion by creating the header and footer files for the template.

Header & Footer

While these are also relatively easy conversions, there are a few things we need to keep in mind with each template; Let's start with the header first. What we're going to do is look at all four of our HTML files to see where they begin to diverge. Once we find the point at which the HTML begins to differ, we'll stop and consider everything before that point our header. In this case, it looks like that happens around line 41, where we begin to define the main content area.

---

[20] If I haven't mentioned this yet, the Codex is your best friend for development.

Converting HTML to a WordPress Theme

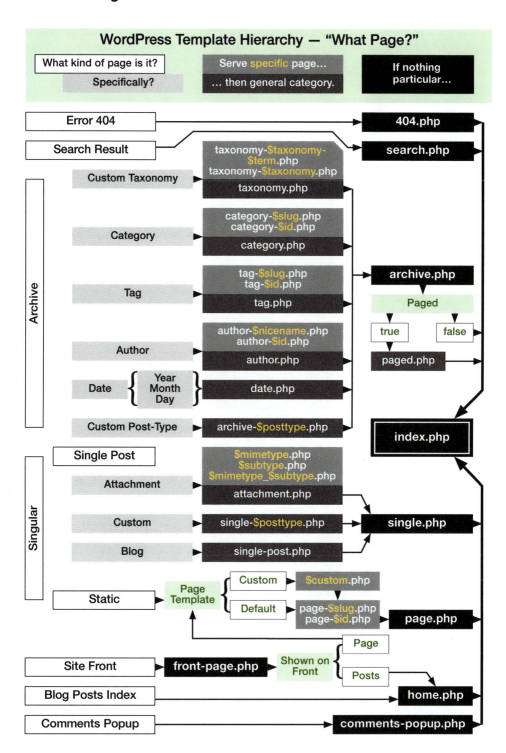

30   **Converting HTML to a WordPress Theme**

```
1   <!DOCTYPE HTML>
2   <html>
3   <head>
4       <title>Director Theme</title>
5       <meta http-equiv="Content-Type" content="text/html; charset=UTF-8" />
6
7       <!--[if lt IE 9]> <script src="http://html5shim.googlecode.com/svn/trunk/html5.js"></script> <![endif]-->
8
9       <link rel="stylesheet" type="text/css" media="screen, projection" href="css/style.css" />
10
11  </head>
12
13  <body>
14
15      <div id="wrap">
16          <div id="container" class="group">
17              <!--Header - Name of Item Here-->
18              <header class="group">
19                  <h1><img src="img/logo.png" alt="Director" /></h1>
20
21                  <div class="searchbar">
22                      <form name="search" method="get" action"/">
23                          <input type="text" name="s" value="Search..." />
24                          <input type="submit" name="submit" value="Search!" />
25                      </form>
26                  </div>
27
28                  <nav>
29                      <ul>
30                          <li><a href="#">Home</a></li>
31                          <li><a href="#">Directory</a></li>
32                          <li><a href="#">Blog</a></li>
33                      </ul>
34                  </nav>
35
36              </header>
37
38              <!-- End Header -->
39
40              <!-- Main Area -->
41              <div id="content" class="group">
```

That means, for starters, that we'll copy everything from line 41 up and add it to a new file that we'll create in the *director/* theme called **header.php**. At this point, the **header.php** file should look exactly like the screenshot above. Now, we'll start WordPress-ifying[21] it. We'll take it a section at a time, starting with the head. This is what we have currently:

```
<head>
    <title>Director Theme</title>
    <meta http-equiv="Content-Type" content="text/html;
      charset=UTF-8" />

    <!--[if lt IE 9]> <script src="http://html5shim.      ►
      googlecode.com/svn/trunk/html5.js"></script>
      <![endif]-->
    <link rel="stylesheet" type="text/css" media="screen,
      projection" href="css/style.css" />

</head>
```

---

[21] Dibs if this is not a real word.

Converting HTML to a WordPress Theme

31

There are a couple of things that we're going to need to replace or add. First, we'll want to replace our title with something more dynamic:

```
<title><?php bloginfo('name'); ?> | <?php wp_title(); ?>
  </title>
```

The first function listed, **bloginfo('name')**, will grab the name of the blog as defined on the *Settings* ➤ *General* page of the Word-Press admin. **wp_title()** will grab the name of the page or post.

Next, we will properly link to the stylesheet and add a trackback (or pingback URL) for when other websites link to us:

```
<link rel="stylesheet" href="<?php bloginfo('stylesheet_   ▶
  url'); ?>" type="text/css" media="screen" />
<link rel="pingback" href="<?php bloginfo('pingback_url');
  ?>" />
```

We're using **bloginfo()** again to grab those values. The last thing we need to do in the head is the most important part. This will allow us to use any hooks and filters that use the **wp_head** hook;[22] essentially, it makes theme additions and plugins work.

```
<?php wp_head(); ?>
```

So with that important final line, we're done customizing the **head**, which should look like this:

```
<head>
  <title><?php bloginfo('name'); ?> | <?php wp_title(); ?>
    </title>
  <meta http-equiv="Content-Type" content="text/html;
    charset=UTF-8" />
  <!--[if lt IE 9]> <script src="http://html5shim.          ▶
    googlecode.com/svn/trunk/html5.js"></script>
    <![endif]-->
```

---

[22] More on that in "Setting up the Custom Post Type."

32   **Converting HTML to a WordPress Theme**

```
<link rel="stylesheet" href="<?php bloginfo('stylesheet_ ▸
    url'); ?>" type="text/css" media="screen" />
<link rel="pingback" href="<?php bloginfo('pingback_    ▸
    url'); ?>" />

<?php wp_head(); ?>

</head>
```

Next up is the `<header>` section, which currently looks like this:

```
<header class="group">
  <h1><img src="images/logo.png" alt="Director" /></h1>

  <div class="searchbar">
    <form name="search" method="get" action="/">
      <input type="text" name="s" value="Search..." />
      <input type="submit" name="submit" value="Search!" />
    </form>
  </div>

  <nav>
    <ul>
      <li><a href="#">Home</a></li>
      <li><a href="#">Directory</a></li>
      <li><a href="#">Blog</a></li>
    </ul>
  </nav>

</header>
```

We're going to change three sections: the `<h1>` contents, the search bar, and the navigation. Since we're actually going to use the *images/* folder now, go ahead and add that to the *director/* folder.

So, first we'll change the heading so that it accurately grabs both the title and the source for the logo:

```
<h1><img src="<?php print IMAGES; ?>/logo.png" alt="<?php
    bloginfo('name'); ?>" /></h1>
```

Converting HTML to a WordPress Theme   **33**

You should notice two things here. The first is that we're using the `IMAGES` constant that we set up in `functions.php`. This pulls the full images path, so all we need to do is tack on the actual file name. Next, we once again use `bloginfo()` to grab the alternate text, which should also be the title of the site in this case.

Next, we're going to make the search bar more dynamic. Let's start by copying the search bar information:

```
<div class="searchbar">
  <form name="search" method="get" action="/">
    <input type="text" name="s" value="Search..." />
    <input type="submit" name="submit" value="Search!" />
  </form>
</div>
```

Paste the above HTML into a file in the */director/* folder that we'll call `searchform.php`. Now we can use a simple function call — `get_search_form()` — anywhere in our theme. The Search widget will use the same template. One more thing we should do (though it's not always necessary) is change the form "action" from "/" to `<?php bloginfo('url'); ?>`. This will ensure our search always calls the blog's homepage. If it doesn't, the search will not work.

Now we can replace the code above with this single line:

```
<?php get_search_form(); ?>
```

Much easier, right? Our final step will be to replace the nav, making it more dynamic; we'll make it so users can update the site navigation from within WordPress. Here's what the new nav section looks like:

```
<?php wp_nav_menu( array('menu' => 'Main', 'container' =>
  'nav' )); ?>
```

The function used to print the site navigation as defined in Word-Press is `wp_nav_menu()`, which can accept several arguments.

34   **Converting HTML to a WordPress Theme**

Most have to do with displaying the menu, which by default prints it in an unordered list. This, as well as `class`, `container`, `id`, and more, are all changeable using the arguments defined in the Word-Press Codex.[23] You'll notice we took advantage of the `container` argument to print our `<nav>` and `</nav>` tags. We could also apply a class or ID using the `container_class` or `container_id` arguments, respectively. The other argument that we use in our theme, `menu`, is used to identify which menu to use, as WordPress allows for the creation of multiple menus. `menu` can accept ID,[24] slug, or name. We defined the latter two in our `functions.php` file; "main" is the slug and "Main Nav" is the name.

And with that, our header is complete. Let's take a look at what we have now:

```
<header class="group">
  <h1><img src="<?php print IMAGES; ?>/logo.png" alt=    ▶
    "<?php bloginfo('name'); ?>" /></h1>

  <?php get_search_form(); ?>

  <?php wp_nav_menu( array('menu' => 'Main', 'container'
    => 'nav' )); ?>
</header>
```

As you can see, we've saved quite a bit of room and have made that section **much** more dynamic. On the following page you'll see a screenshot of the entire header, line count and all. Now, let's take care of our footer.

Let's go back to our HTML templates and see what we should copy into the footer. Since our header ends with opening a `<div>` with the ID of "content", we should definitely start the footer by closing that. Luckily, I've placed comments in my code marking the beginning and end of important sections. If we look at `index.html`,

---

[23] http://codex.wordpress.org/Function_Reference/wp_nav_menu

[24] Which you can select from the WordPress admin.

Converting HTML to a WordPress Theme

35

```
1   <!DOCTYPE HTML>
2   <html>
3   <head>
4       <title><?php bloginfo('name'); ?> | <?php wp_title(); ?></title>
5       <meta http-equiv="Content-Type" content="text/html; charset=UTF-8" />
6
7       <!--[if lt IE 9]> <script src="http://html5shim.googlecode.com/svn/trunk/html5.js"></script> <![endif]-->
8
9       <link rel="stylesheet" href="<?php bloginfo('stylesheet_url'); ?>" type="text/css" media="screen" />
10      <link rel="pingback" href="<?php bloginfo('pingback_url'); ?>" />
11
12      <?php wp_head(); ?>
13
14  </head>
15  |
16  <body>
17
18      <div id="wrap">
19          <div id="container" class="group">
20              <!--Header - Name of Item Here-->
21              <header class="group">
22                  <h1><img src="<?php print IMAGES; ?>/logo.png" alt="<?php bloginfo('name'); ?>" /></h1>
23
24                  <?php get_search_form(); ?>
25
26                  <?php wp_nav_menu( array('menu' => 'Main', 'container' => 'nav' )); ?>
27
28              </header>
29
30              <!-- End Header -->
31              <hr/>
32              <!-- Main Area -->
33              <div id="content" class="group">
```

Over 10 lines less! Not too shabby.

we'll see that the footer code starts on line 103 and goes until the end of the `index.html` file:

```
102
103                 </div>  <!-- End Main Area -->
104
105         </div>
106         <!--end container-->
107     </div>
108
109     <!--Footer Information-->
110     <footer class="group">
111
112         <p>&copy; SiteName, Year. All Rights Reserved</p>
113     </footer>
114     <!-- End Footer Information -->
115
116 </body>
117 </html>
118
```

Let's create `footer.php` in the */director/* folder and copy that code into it. As for making it WordPress-friendly, there is actually very little that we need to do, so we're going to take care of it all at once, in line order.

On line 10 of our new footer file, you'll see the copyright line is very static. We'll want to use the actual name of the site, as well as give it an actual year. So let's replace that line with this:

36   **Converting HTML to a WordPress Theme**

```
<p>&copy; <?php bloginfo('name'); ?>, <?=date('Y');?>. All
    Rights Reserved</p>
```

We used **bloginfo()** for the name, and the standard **date()** function[25] to grab the current year — that way, we don't have to update the template every January.

Aside from that, there is only one thing left to do. Right before the **</body>** tag, add this:

```
<?php wp_footer(); ?>
```

Much like **wp_head** in our **header.php** file, this will fire the **wp_footer** hook, calling any plugins that add functionality to the footer. Our entire footer should look like this (again, in screenshot form):

```
 1  </div>  <!-- End Main Area -->
 2
 3          </div>
 4          <!--end container-->
 5      </div>
 6
 7      <!--Footer Information-->
 8      <footer class="group">
 9
10          <p>&copy; <?php bloginfo('name'); ?>, <?=date('Y');?>. All Rights Reserved</p>
11      </footer>
12      <!-- End Footer Information -->
13
14
15      <?php wp_footer(); ?>
16
17  </body>
18  </html>
```

Eighteen lines and not too much customization — looks pretty good to me.

Now that we've got the header and footer, it's time to get into the red meat of the theme — the posts and pages! Before we do that, however, I need to tell you about the famous[26] WordPress Loop.

---

[25] http://php.net/manual/en/function.date.php

[26] Actually famous.

Converting HTML to a WordPress Theme **37**

The Loop

Oh the Loop; it's a living, breathing thing. It's the backbone of WordPress — what makes everything tick. Without the Loop, there would be no dynamic content.[27] Using the Loop, we can print any content, however we want. Who would be better to describe the Loop than the actual makers? Here's what the WordPress Codex has to say about the Loop:[28]

> ❝ *The Loop is used by WordPress to display each of your posts. Using the Loop, WordPress processes each of the posts to be displayed on the current page and formats them according to how they match specified criteria within the Loop tags. Any HTML or PHP code placed in the Loop will be repeated on each post.* ❞

Essentially, WordPress has a set of tags to: a) make sure that we have posts to display, and b) display those posts. The tags, called Template Tags,[29] allow us to fully customize how we display the information from each post.

We start off the Loop this way:

```php
<?php if ( have_posts() ) : while ( have_posts() ) :
    the_post(); ?>
```

Three things are happening here:

1. `have_posts()` is making sure there are posts to display.

2. The same function will continually keep track of whether we still have posts, which is why it's used as the while condition

3. `the_post()` unpacks the next post in the queue.

---

[27] Well, very little anyway.

[28] http://codex.wordpress.org/The_Loop

[29] http://codex.wordpress.org/Template_Tags

38   Converting HTML to a WordPress Theme

WordPress automatically grabs the posts by querying the database based on the URL. You could also overwrite the original query by using `WP_Query()` or `query_posts()` to get your own information. In any case, as long as that query returns posts, `have_posts()` returns true and we enter the Loop. We end the Loop with this:

```
<?php endwhile; else: ?>
<p><?php _e('No posts were found. Sorry!'); ?></p>
<?php endif; ?>
```

We end the Loop and have a simple fallback here, in the case that `have_posts()` returns false, that tells the user we have no posts for them. Inside the Loop, we can do all kinds of things to completely customize the post display. While I won't go through all of the Template Tags, I will point out some of the most commonly used ones. All of the following functions print out their value by default.[30] Some of these functions also accept Boolean values, which determine if the value should be printed or returned.

- `the_title()` – Gets the title of the post or page. It accepts three arguments: HTML tag for before the title (named `$before`), HTML tag for after the title (named `$after`), and `$echo`, the actual title itself.

- `the_time()` – Gets the date the post or page was published. The only argument it accepts is the format in which that the date should be printed. These arguments are the same ones that the PHP date function[31] accepts. The default is whatever is listed in the WordPress admin panel, under *Settings* ➤ *General*.

- `the_content()` – This will display the content of the post or page (that is, whatever you entered as the body text in the visual editor of the WordPress admin. It accepts two arguments, the first of which tells WordPress what to display as

---

[30] Each of these tags has a corresponding function prepended with `get_` (e.g. `get_the_title`) that will return the value instead of printing it.

[31] http://php.net/manual/en/function.date.php

Converting HTML to a WordPress Theme

the "more" text. I'll talk about this at length in the next section. The second argument, called `$stripteaser` is simply documented as a Boolean that will, "Strip teaser content before the "more" text."[32] There are no examples on the Codex, and there is some debate over what it actually does.

- `the_excerpt()` – Gets the first 55 words of the post, appending " […] " to the end of the string. It accepts no arguments. Both the number of words and the ellipsis (…) can be changed within the functions file using filters.

- `the_category()` – Gets the category (or categories) in which the posts are listed. For arguments, it accepts: the separator, which will be printed in between categories, how to handle displaying parent categories, and the post ID, which of course defaults to the current post.

- `the_tags()` – Gets the tags added to the post. The arguments it accepts are: what to print before the list of tags, how to separate each tag, and what to print after each tag.

- `the_permalink()` – Gets the post's or page's URL in the format defined by the WordPress admin panel in *Settings* ➤ *Permalinks*.

You can write an entire book on WordPress' template tags for techniques inside and outside of the Loop;[33] I just wanted to familiarize you with some of the more common ones that will appear in this book.

The Post Pages

The Index

Now that we are Loop experts, let's create some pages that use it, starting with `index.php`. As you know from the template hierarchy,

---

[32] http://codex.wordpress.org/Function_Reference/the_content#Parameters

[33] Someone probably did.

40   **Converting HTML to a WordPress Theme**

`index.php` is the fallback template for all of the other WordPress template pages; it would make sense to develop this one first. Create an `index.php` file in your *director/* theme. The first thing we should do is include the header and footer in the file using the `get_header()` and `get_footer()` template tags. This is what our entire `index.php` file should look like right now:

```php
<?php get_header(); ?>

<?php get_footer(); ?>
```

Now, let's open up `blog.html` and see how we want our posts to be displayed. We want to cut out everything that we've already included in `header.php` and `footer.php`, which leaves us with this:

```html
<div id="main" class="group">
    <div id="blog" class="left-col">
        <div class="post">
            <h2>Morbi leo risus, porta ac consectetur</h2>
            <div class="byline">by <a href="#">HAROLD OVERMAN</a> on <a href="#">THURSDAY, JANUARY 12, 2012</a></div>

            <p>Ac, vestibulum at eros. Praesent commodo cursus magna, vel scelerisque nisl consectetur et. Maecenas faucibus mollis interdum. Lorem ipsum dolor sit amet, consectetur adipiscing elit. Duis mollis, est non commodo luctus, nisi erat porttitor ligula, eget lacinia odio sem nec elit. Nullam quis risus eget urna mollis ornare el eu leo. Nullam id dolor id nibh ultricies vehicula ut id elit.</p>
        </div>

        <div class="post">
            <h2>Morbi leo risus, porta ac consectetur</h2>
            <div class="byline">by <a href="#">HAROLD OVERMAN</a> on <a href="#">THURSDAY, JANUARY 12, 2012</a></div>

            <p>Ac, vestibulum at eros. Praesent commodo cursus magna, vel scelerisque nisl consectetur et. Maecenas faucibus mollis interdum. Lorem ipsum dolor sit amet, consectetur adipiscing elit. Duis mollis, est non commodo luctus, nisi erat porttitor ligula, eget lacinia odio sem nec elit. Nullam quis risus eget urna mollis ornare el eu leo. Nullam id dolor id nibh ultricies vehicula ut id elit.</p>
        </div>

        <div class="navi">
            <div class="right">
                <a href="#">Previous</a> / <a href="#">Next</a>
            </div>

            <ul class="pages">
                <li>Page</li>
                <li><a href="#">1</a></li>
                <li>2</li>
                <li><a href="#">3</a></li>
                <li><a href="#">4</a></li>
                <li><a href="#">5</a></li>
                <li><a href="#">6</a></li>
                <li><a href="#">7</a></li>
            </ul>
        </div>

    </div>
    <aside class="right-col">
        <div class="widget">
            <h3>ABOUT US</h3>
            <p>Ac, vestibulum at eros. Praesent commodo cursus magna, vel scelerisque nisl consectetur et. Maecenas faucibus mollis interdum. Lorem ipsum dolor sit amet, consectetur adipiscing elit.</p>

            <p>Vestibulum id ligula porta felis euismod semper. Curabitur blandit tempus porttitor. Praesent commodo cursus magna, vel scelerisque nisl consectetur et.</p>

            <p><a href="#">MORE ABOUT US...</a></p>
        </div>
    </aside>
</div>
```

Copy and paste that code in between the `get_header()` and `get_footer()` tags. Converting this will be a little more difficult because we will need to determine what belongs in the Loop and what does not, as well as separate out our sidebar, which belongs in its own template.

Converting HTML to a WordPress Theme

41

We can tell what should go in the Loop based on what's repeating in the mock-up; here, you can see anything in-between `<div class="post">` and the corresponding `</div>` belong within the Loop. Armed with that knowledge, let's get the `index.php` template in order. Anything above our first `<div class="post">` tag goes before the Loop, so the top[34] of `index.php` looks like this:

```
<?php get_header(); ?>
<div id="main" class="group">
  <div id="blog" class="left-col">
```

That's easy enough! Now let's get started on that Loop. We will start it the same way you start every Loop:

```
<?php if ( have_posts() ) : while ( have_posts() ) :
  the_post(); ?>
```

Now, we'll use our mock-up as a guide for filling in the template tags. We're going to add the following tags inside the Loop: `the_title()`, `the_date()`, `the_author_posts_link()`, and `the_content()`. We will also get rid of each repeating post `<div>`, since we'll only need to print the post once. Replace lines 5-19 with the following code:

```
<div class="post">
<h2><a href="<?php the_permalink(); ?>"><?php the_title();
  ?></a></h2>
  <div class="byline">by <?php the_author_posts_link(); ?>
    on <a href="<?php the_permalink(); ?>"><?php the_time( ▸
    'l F d, Y'); ?></a></div>
  <?php the_content('Read More...'); ?>
</div>
```

You should recognize most of what we see here from earlier in this book, under "The Loop." One template tag that I didn't explain before is `the_author_posts_link()`, which is a function that

---

[34] That is, everything before the Loop.

42   **Converting HTML to a WordPress Theme**

prints the author's display name[35] as a link to all of his or her posts. It accepts no arguments. I also want to take this opportunity to talk about `the_content()`'s `$more_link_text` parameter.

As you might know, in the WordPress editor, you can add `<!--more-->` into a post as a way to identify teaser text or an intro paragraph for your post. The first argument of `the_content()` gets appended to only have content above the `<!--more-->` tag. Of course, this will only happen on pages designed to show multiple posts. On the `single.php` template, the entire post will be displayed.

With that last addition, we now have the entire contents of our Loop. Now it's time to close it out[36] using the same code that I mentioned above. Place it right after the `</div>` that closes out the post div:

```php
<?php endwhile; else: ?>
<p><?php _e('No posts were found. Sorry!'); ?></p>
<?php endif; ?>
```

With the Loop finished, let's move onto the page navigation. Right now, we have the previous and next links hard coded:

```html
<div class="navi">
  <div class="right">
    <a href="#">Previous</a> / <a href="#">Next</a>
  </div>
</div>
```

This is easy enough to replace with dynamic links, as WordPress has native template tags for this information. We'll just replace that code with:

```html
<div class="navi">
  <div class="right">
```

---

[35] Configurable in the WordPress admin area under *Users*.

Converting HTML to a WordPress Theme

43

```
            <?php previous_posts_link('Previous'); ?> / <?php
                next_posts_link('Next'); ?>
        </div>
    </div>
```

Both `previous_posts_link` and `next_posts_link` work outside the Loop and will link to the previous and next post pages. They accept as their first argument any string that you want displayed as the link. There is also an optional second argument in which you can define the maximum number of pages the next/previous links are displayed. There is by default, no limit. It's worth noting again, these refer to the order of the pages, not the order of the posts. "Next" will take you to older posts, and vise versa for "Previous."

This is the last bit of content in the larger left column of our template. After closing out the main `<div>` with `</div>`, it's time to move on to the sidebar. For now, we're going to cut and paste the entire sidebar into its own template file and worry about making it dynamic later. Cut everything from the start of your HTML file's sidebar to the end of it, and paste it into a new file named `sidebar.php`. Now add the following to where our sidebar was (around line 25):

```
    <?php get_sidebar(); ?>
```

Perfect! Now to close out the "main" `<div>` and finish `index.php`:

```
    </div>
```

We now have a fully functional WordPress theme! Of course, we're going to make some more customizations to it. As for `index.php`, that should now look like this (top of page 44).

It's a perfect copy of our mock-up, with our own blog content![37]

---

[36] Unless you want things to be really, really broken.

[37] Or in this case, content from wpcandy (http://wpcandy.com/made/the-sample-post-collection).

44 Converting HTML to a WordPress Theme

```php
<?php get_header(); ?>

<div id="main" class="group">
    <div id="blog" class="left-col">

        <?php if (have_posts()) : while (have_posts()) : the_post(); ?>

        <div class="post">
            <h2><a href="<?php the_permalink(); ?>"><?php the_title(); ?></a></h2>
            <div class="byline">by <?php the_author_posts_link(); ?> on <a href="<?php the_permalink(); ?>"><?php the_time('l F d, Y'); ?></a></div>
                <?php the_content('Read More...'); ?>
        </div>

        <?php endwhile; else: ?>
            <p><?php _e('No posts were found. Sorry!'); ?></p>
        <?php endif; ?>

        <div class="navi">
            <div class="right">
                <?php previous_posts_link('Previous'); ?> / <?php next_posts_link('Next'); ?>
            </div>
        </div>

    </div>
    <?php get_sidebar(); ?>
</div>

<?php get_footer(); ?>
```

Our revised `index.php` *file.*

The index page in action matches our mockup.

Single Page Template

Next, we'll create the `single.php` template, which is designed to display a single post. Admittedly, it won't be much different from our `index.php` template. I do want to illustrate the small differences between the two, as well as the template hierarchy. Go ahead and add a `single.php` file the */director/* folder, and copy the contents of `index.php` into it.

Converting HTML to a WordPress Theme

45

One of the changes we are going to make is to remove the permalink references, since we are now on that post's page. There are currently two, for the title and the date. We should replace this code:

```
<h2><a href="<?php the_permalink(); ?>"><?php the_title();
  ?></a></h2>
<div class="byline">by <?php the_author_posts_link(); ?>
  on <a href="<?php the_permalink(); ?>"><?php the_time(  ▶
  'l F d, Y'); ?></a></div>
```

With this:

```
<h2><?php the_title(); ?></h2>
<div class="byline">by <?php the_author_posts_link(); ?>
  on <span class="date"><?php the_time('l F d, Y'); ?></a>  ▶
  </div>
```

Notice that in order to keep consistent styling for the date, we wrapped it in a span element with the class of "date".

Next, we'll want to change the post navigation to move to the next or previous post, not the next of previous **page** of posts. Two things need to happen. We need to:

- Move the "navi" section inside the Loop.

- Replace the current, previous, and next functions with ones that will display posts instead of pages.

Copy the following code and place it right above **endwhile;** — right before the end of the Loop:

```
<div class="navi">
  <div class="right">
    <?php previous_posts_link('Previous'); ?> / <?php
      next_posts_link('Next'); ?>
  </div>
</div>
```

46 Converting HTML to a WordPress Theme

Now we'll replace `previous_posts_link()` and `next_posts_link()` with `previous_post_link()` and `next_post_link()` respectively. While there isn't much difference in their names (besides a single "s"), the latter two accept a few more arguments and are very flexible.[38] Because of that, we'll also want to remove the arguments `'Previous'` (from `previous_post_link()`) and `'Next'` (from `next_post_link()`). Now by default, they will display the title of the next/previous post as a link, which is exactly what we're looking for. What we have now is simply:

```
<div class="navi">
  <div class="right">
    <?php previous_post_link(); ?> / <?php next_post_
      link(); ?>
  </div>
</div>
```

That will give us this:

AN ORDERED LIST POST
by **JOE CASABONA** *on WEDNESDAY SEPTEMBER 17, 2008*

Nulla sagittis convallis arcu. Sed sed nunc. Curabitur consequat. Quisque metus enim, venenatis fermentum, mollis in, porta et, nibh. Duis vulputate elit in elit. Mauris dictum libero id justo. Fusce in est. Sed nec diam. Pellentesque habitant morbi tristique senectus et netus et malesuada fames ac turpis egestas. Quisque semper nibh eget nibh. Sed tempor. Fusce erat.

An Ordered List

1. Vestibulum in mauris semper tortor interdum ultrices.

2. Sed vel lorem et justo laoreet bibendum. Donec dictum.

3. Etiam massa libero, lacinia at, commodo in, tincidunt a, purus.

4. Praesent volutpat eros quis enim blandit tincidunt.

5. Aenean eu libero nec lectus ultricies laoreet. Donec rutrum, nisi vel egestas ultrices, ipsum urna sagittis libero, vitae vestibulum dui dolor vel velit.

« A SIMPLE TEXT POST / ANOTHER POST WITH EVERYTHING IN IT »

If we'd like, we could also add the categories and tags using the template tags mentioned earlier. Just amend the byline `div` to read like this:

[38] http://codex.wordpress.org/Function_Reference/next_post_link

Converting HTML to a WordPress Theme

47

```
<div class="byline">
  by <?php the_author_posts_link(); ?> on <span class=
    "date"><?php the_time('l F d, Y'); ?></span><br/>
  Posted in: <?php the_category(', '); ?> | <?php
    the_tags('Tagged with: ', ', '); ?>
</div>
```

That code will result in this byline:

AN ORDERED LIST POST
by **JOE CASABONA** *on WEDNESDAY SEPTEMBER 17, 2008*
Posted in: **NEWS, UNCATEGORIZED** | *Tagged with:* **LIST, ORDERED, TEST**

While this is all the customization that I'm going to make to `single.php`, you don't have to stop here. `single.php` a great template to experiment with. Then again, so is the next one.

Content Pages

What really brought WordPress to the next level as a platform was the ability to create pages that were separate from traditional blog posts. It went from being simply a blogging platform to being a CMS. We are going to harness that power to create a page template designed specifically to display page content.

Once again, there won't be too many differences between this template and `index.php` or `single.php`, but there are some noteworthy adjustments that we need to make.

- What's often referred to the "post meta data" (author, categories, tags, etc.) are not important on pages, so we can remove them.

- Similarly, when traversing through pages, we can safely assume the user will look to the site's navigation. We can remove the previous and next post functions.

Go ahead and create a new file in the */director/* folder named `page.php` and copy the contents of `single.php` into it. Once we do that, we will simple remove the following two sections:

48   **Converting HTML to a WordPress Theme**

```html
<div class="byline">
  by <?php the_author_posts_link(); ?> on <span class=       ▶
    "date"><?php the_time('l F d, Y'); ?></span><br/>
  Posted in: <?php the_category(', '); ?> | <?php
    the_tags('Tagged with: ', ', '); ?>
</div>
```

and

```html
<div class="navi">
  <div class="right">
    <?php previous_post_link(); ?> / <?php next_post_       ▶
      link(); ?>
  </div>
</div>
```

That leaves our Loop looking very lean:

```php
<?php if (have_posts()) : while (have_posts()) :
  the_post(); ?>
  <div class="post group">
    <h2><?php the_title(); ?></h2>
    <?php the_content('Read More...'); ?>
  </div>
<?php endwhile; else: ?>
<p><?php _e('No posts were found. Sorry!'); ?></p>
<?php endif; ?>
```

Save it, and we're done! The top of page 49 (following) shows what the resulting pages look like.

It is worth noting that since posts and pages are inherently the same, most template tags for posts behave the same way for pages. The obvious exceptions are `the_category()` and `the_tags()`, since you cannot assign either to pages in WordPress.

With these template files, we have several unique displays that will allow the user to differentiate between post listings, single posts,

Converting HTML to a WordPress Theme

and pages. Since we did not create custom search or archive templates, they will default to `index.php`. For this theme, that is fine. There is one page that we haven't created yet, however, and that's our custom homepage. This will have to wait until after we create our plugin, since the homepage relies on that.

There are also several auxiliary template pages that we haven't customized/created yet. In the next section, we'll create templates for the sidebar, archives, and 404 errors.

Auxiliary Template Pages

These pages are important because we can distinguish them from the rest of the theme. There are fewer dependencies, which means less to change, which means more customization. Let's start with the `sidebar.php` template page that we've already created.

The Sidebar Template

Our sidebar template (`sidebar.php`) as it stands now looks like this:

```
<aside class="right-col">
  <div class="widget">
    <h3>ABOUT US</h3>
```

50   Converting HTML to a WordPress Theme

```html
        <p>Ac, vestibulum at eros. Praesent commodo cursus
          magna, vel scelerisque nisl consectetur et. Maecenas
          faucibus mollis interdum. Lorem ipsum dolor sit amet,
          consectetur adipiscing elit.</p>

        <p>Vestibulum id ligula porta felis euismod semper.
          Curabitur blandit tempus porttitor. Praesent commodo
          cursus magna, vel scelerisque nisl consectetur et.
          </p>
        <p><a href="#">MORE ABOUT US...</a></p>
      </div>
    </aside>
```

We actually aren't too far off from what we want here. Remember, back in our functions file, we defined a sidebar named "Primary Sidebar." After the `<aside>` tag, we're going to make sure that sidebar exists.

```php
    <?php if ( !function_exists( 'dynamic_sidebar' ) ||
      !dynamic_sidebar('Primary Sidebar') ) : ?>
```

The code above is saying "if Primary Sidebar does not exist, print the following." Now we can throw `<?php endif; ?>` right before `</aside>` and be done, but we probably want to put something useful there, in the case that either: no dynamic sidebar is defined, or the user has not defined a sidebar. I usually like to include a searchbar:

```php
    <div class="widget">
      <h3>Search</h3>
      <?php get_search_form(); ?>
    </div>
```

Remember that while the sidebar we defined does include all of the markup for us, we still need to write in a fallback. Now we're ready to close the conditional statement. Our entire `sidebar.php` file looks like this:

Converting HTML to a WordPress Theme

```
<aside class="right-col">
  <?php if ( !function_exists( 'dynamic_sidebar' ) ||
    !dynamic_sidebar('Primary Sidebar') ) : ?>
    <div class="widget">
      <h3>Search</h3>
      <?php get_search_form(); ?>
    </div>
  <?php endif; ?>
</aside>
```

And, if you'd like to see what it looks like (left is by default, right is with some widgets):

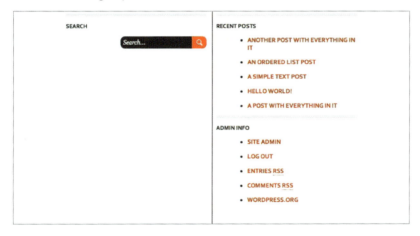

We can also create multiple sidebars fairly easily. We would just create a new template page called `sidebar-other.php` using similar code to what's in `sidebar.php`. Instead of checking `!dynamic_sidebar('Primary Sidebar')`, we would simply check `!dynamic_sidebar('Other')` and define `Other` in our `functions.php` file, as we did with Primary Sidebar. The final piece of the puzzle comes when calling that `get_sidebar()` in the template. As I explained earlier, instead of just calling `get_sidebar()`, we would pass an argument, explicitly telling WordPress what sidebar template we want to use. In this case, it would be `get_sidebar('other')`.

Archives Template

Next up, we're going to create a general archives page. You should note that this will display links to month and category archives, not actual posts, which could be done by creating an `archive.php` template page. However, our `index.php` template is handling that. Also, this is going to be a page template so we'll need to create a page in WordPress that uses the template. WordPress does not have a reserved "Archives" page template.

Create a file named **page-archives.php**[39] and place it in the */director/* theme. Next, we'll start the file off with this text:

```
<?php
/*
* Template Name: Archives
*/
?>
<?php get_header(); ?>
<div id="main" class="group">
  <div id="blog" class="left-col archives">
```

Our first few lines tell WordPress that this is a page template named "Archives," which WordPress will use when a user is creating or editing a page. The rest should look familiar since it's everything before the Loop on the **page.php** template, with the addition of the CSS class `.archives` after `.left-col`. This will apply some special CSS to our archives page.

Next, we'll want to add in the information for our archives. Since we're not pulling any direct content from WordPress, we do not need the Loop. Instead, we'll be using two other template tags:

- `wp_get_archives()` – This will return a list of posts organized by date, based on the value of an argument named "type". The value can be: `daily`, `weekly`, `monthly`, `yearly`,

---

[39] In some themes, developers will just name this `archives.php`. I'm following the convention that any page template has the prefix `page-`.

Converting HTML to a WordPress Theme

53

postbypost, and `alpha`. The only difference between `postbypost` and `alpha` is that `postbypost` sorts by date, and `alpha` sorts by title.[40]

- `wp_list_categories()` – This function will return a list of category links based on the criteria you send it. You can customize things like which categories to display, how to display them, if you want to include a count, and more.[41]

We're going to use these with what are mostly the default settings. Starting on the next line of `archives.php`, add this:

```
<h2>Archives by Month:</h2>
  <ul>
    <?php wp_get_archives('type=monthly'); ?>
  </ul>

<h2>Archives by Subject:</h2>
  <ul>
    <?php wp_list_categories('hierarchical=0&title_li='); ?>
  </ul>
```

As you can see, we aren't using too many custom settings for either function here. With `wp_get_archives()`, we're calling the monthly archives, and for the rest, we are using the defaults.[42] With `wp_list_categories()`, again, we are primarily using the default settings. However, we are making a couple of notable changes. The first is that we aren't displaying the categories hierarchically. By default, child categories would display as nested unordered lists under their parents. For display purposes, we've set this to `false` (or 0). There is also an argument called `title_li`. By default this argument will make the first list item the title (which is "Categories" unless otherwise noted) and make all of the categories a nested list. By setting `title_li` to nothing, the categories become the top-level list.

---

[40] http://codex.wordpress.org/Template_Tags/wp_get_archives

[41] http://codex.wordpress.org/Template_Tags/wp_list_categories

We're going to round out our template using the same familiar:

```
    </div>
    <?php get_sidebar(); ?>
</div>
<?php get_footer(); ?>
```

We're done with the `page-archives.php` template! Once you create a page in the WordPress admin panel and apply the Archive template, you will end up with something like this:

The 404 Error Template

Unlike the archive template, our 404 page is not one we need to create in WordPress.[43] We'll simply create a file named `404.php` and add it to our /director/ folder. This is going to be a somewhat stripped down version of the rest of the pages. It will include some text, a silly image, and no sidebar. We're starting with this:

```
<?php get_header(); ?>
<div id="main" class="group fourohfour">
```

Pretty standard stuff, except you'll notice that we've again applied a custom class to our page. The only thing `.fourohfour` does in the CSS is center all of the text. Next we'll add in our content:

---

[42] Actually, monthly is the default type too, but I wanted to illustrate sending at least one argument to the function.

[43] That would be kind of weird, considering 404 is "Page not Found."

Converting HTML to a WordPress Theme   55

```
<h2>404: Page not Found!?</h2>

<img class="aligncenter" src="<?php print IMAGES;?>/404.
  jpg" alt="404'd!"/>

  <p>I am just as surprised as you are! Maybe we should
    just move along back to the <a href="<?php
    bloginfo('home'); ?>">homepage</a>.</p>
```

Here's our page. Just a heading, an image, and some text redirecting the user back to the homepage.[44] After that, we simply close out the template:

```
</div>
<?php get_footer(); ?>
```

Then save it, and you're done! You now have a custom 404 page. Go to a nonexistent page that you know won't work and you will see this:[45]

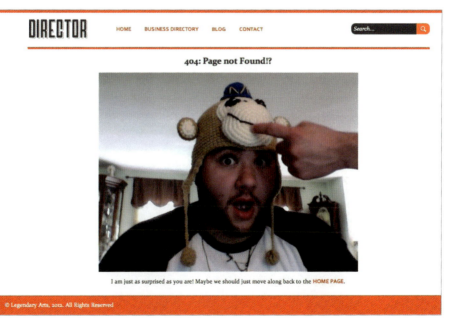

---

[44] You, of course, can do more. Here are some awesome 404 pages: http://list25.com/25-creatively-awesome-404-pages/

[45] That is one handsome fella.

Building Our Own Framework

I find when building themes, I'm usually starting in the same place every time. Because of this, I started writing blocks of code that I could reuse. One of the best things about my education at the University of Scranton was the recurring lesson we learned about **reuse**. Reuse is incredibly important in programming for many reasons: easier testing, saving time, the ability to focus on more advanced things, etc. Once I graduated and entered the wonderful world of full-time freelancing, I decided that if I was going to keep doing WordPress work, I would need to apply those reuse lessons to my everyday life. The first thing I did was develop those blocks of code into a full blown theme framework.

I want to go over some thoughts about reuse, and coding; these are things you can keep in mind if you decide to build your own framework. I personally think the theme that we just developed is a pretty good starting point.[46]

Principles of Reuse

Anyone with formal education in Computer Science or Software Engineering can attest to the fact that there are countless theories, libraries, and classes (programming classes, not school classes) dedicated to some very advanced forms of reuse and generic programming. While I think those are overkill for the simple theme framework I had in mind, there are some principles I tried to follow:

---

[46] I also have a four-part series on this topic over at WPTuts+: http://wp.tutsplus. com/ series/diy-theme-framework/. Most of this section was taken from the 1st and 2nd articles.

Converting HTML to a WordPress Theme

- **Design Your Code –** I know when talking about WordPress, design usually implies the front-end design, but it's just as important to design the code. Lay out what your functions, classes, and pages will be before you start to code them up.

- **Generalize When Possible –** Possibly the most important principle is to always recognize when you're reusing code snippets and to generalize them into functions. This will make managing and updating your code much, much easier.

- **Document and Test Thoroughly –** This is something you should do with all code, but especially code that you plan on reusing frequently. Documenting will help you remember what you were thinking six months or a year down the line. Testing will ensure your code works before implementing it 5, 10, or 20 times.

Define Your Needs

Now that we've laid out some principles to keep in mind, we need to define what we want our framework to accomplish. Remember, each of us has our own needs, and while I'm going to talk about mine, yours may be different. My needs were fairly simple at first; I wanted a simple framework that did my initial work for me.

While creating WordPress themes for my clients, I noticed my process was the same: copy K2 (the default theme at the time), remove the stuff I didn't want to use, replace it with my code. A lot of my code was similar: the same CSS reset, the same CSS structure, the same style header, navigation, etc. After a while, I found it was easier just to copy my last client's theme and build from that. It was then that I decided to build my own framework.

With that decided, I needed to define my needs: what work I was doing repeatedly, and which parts of that work I could generalize. My list of requirements was as such:

58 Converting HTML to a WordPress Theme

- **Pluggable CSS –** There are several parts of my CSS that rarely change. This includes in WordPress class definitions, my CSS reset, some general classes I use (`.hide`, `.left`, `.right`, `.clear`, etc.), and (usually) my IE Fixes. If I could abstract that all away, all I would need to do is dump in a site-specific CSS file (called `master.css` after Dan Cederholm's simple CSS framework) and I know everything else would work properly.

- **Constants for the Theme URL and Image Paths –** These are two variables I need with every theme. If I could easily define them somewhere, I wouldn't need to worry about replacing the URLs for every site I create. You'll notice I implemented these when creating the `functions.php` file earlier in this book.

- **Common WordPress Functionality –** This is the menus, sidebar definitions, and anything else I could think of that I'd be typing over and over again.

- **Generally Defined Template Pages –** The common theme pages (header, footer, index) with enough on them to make them useful, but not so much on them that I'd have to really change the theme every time I developed a new theme.

- **Common Folders –** I always have an *images* folder, *css* folder, and a *css/img* folder. I had to include these too.

- **Lightweight –** It's got to be lightweight. I don't want to have to sift through pages and pages of code to find what I want. My thought is that WordPress itself is a complex framework; why build a second complex framework on top?

I also wanted to build some functions for features of several pages, like the "page not found message" and the posts page navigation. This goes back to the mentality that a single function will help me more quickly change multi-page features.

Converting HTML to a WordPress Theme 59

If you are going to start with what we've laid out here, make sure to cut away anything you don't think will be useful across all sites and to create functions for what you think you'll use a lot. It's possible that our Loop could be thrown into a function, or the 404 page could be generalized to fit the needs of any site (granted, it's pretty general now). A framework should also include a comments template, especially if you'll be applying it to blogs.[47]

There are some things to keep in mind when coding your framework, especially if you're going to apply it to child themes. My first tip, however, is to see what's already out there.

Existing Theme Frameworks

You don't want to reinvent the wheel. As a matter of fact, the whole idea behind creating a theme framework is to prevent that very thing. So you might as well check out what's already out there. Below are some of the more popular ones I've seen and/or used.

- Thematic
- Thesis
- Carrington
- Genesis
- Atahualpa
- From the WordPress Codex

While exploring these frameworks, keep your requirements in mind. Test these properly: download, install, enable; then try building a child theme and playing with the settings. See what you find, then make your decision.

If you do decide to go the way of coding your own, like I did, there are some things you should keep in mind.

---

[47] To be honest, I usually do not include comments when setting up sites; most of the time it's not something my clients or I want to deal with.

Coding Tips for Frameworks/Child Themes

First, you should know how child themes work when creating your framework. When creating one, the `style.css` file will have the same theme definition, with one additional line:

```
/*
Theme Name:  Child Theme
Theme URI:   http: //example.com/
Description: Child theme for Your Framework Theme
Author:      Your Name
Author URI:  http://your-site.com/
Template:    parent-theme
Version:     1.0
*/
```

The line labeled "Template" will tell WordPress where the child's parent resides. This should match the name of the folder exactly; it is case-sensitive.

Also, regarding the `style.css` file, the child theme will completely overwrite the parent's. That means that none of the CSS from the parent theme will automatically be pulled in to the child theme. In order to grab the CSS from the parent, you'll have to include this line right after the theme definition:

```
@import url("../parent-theme/style.css");
```

You would replace "parent-theme" above with the folder name of your theme's parent theme, of course.

The way WordPress child themes handles the `style.css` file is pretty much the same it handles every template file — the parent file will be overwritten by the child. All other files (that is, ones that do not exist in the child theme) will be imported from the parent theme. There is one exception: `functions.php`.

In the case of the `functions.php` file, the child's version of the file is loaded, followed immediately by the parent's version. This is

Converting HTML to a WordPress Theme 61

great news because the child can use any function you have in the parent. You will need to be careful though; if you have a function in the child theme with the same name as one in the parent theme, you'll get an error (or the parent's function will overwrite the child's). What I recommend doing for your framework, to allow for function customization, is this:

```
if ( ! function_exists( 'this_cool_function' ) ):
  function this_cool_function(){
    //some stuff would probably go here.
  }
endif;
```

What this bit of code is essentially saying is to only create that new function if an identically-named function doesn't already exist. This will prevent any errors or overwrites from happening.

The last thing I want to point out before moving onto Custom Post Types is the difference between `bloginfo('template_directory')` and `bloginfo('stylesheet_directory')`. As you'll recall, when we created our `functions.php` file for the Director theme, we used `stylesheet_directory`. While either would have been fine here, there is a key difference that applies to parent and child themes. With `template_directory`, we'd get the full URL of the parent theme returned. With `stylesheet_directory`, the full URL to the child theme is used instead. That means if we use Director as a parent theme, `template_directory` would grab the wrong path.

If you do decide to create a theme framework, I recommend checking out my 4-part series on WPTuts+, which takes you from planning to development, including a child theme and repurposing the framework, much like a boilerplate. That can be found here: http://wp.tutsplus.com/series/diy-theme-framework/.

Creating Custom Post Types

Quite possibly the best addition to WordPress 3.0 was Custom Post Types. This took WordPress from being a CMS that can manage posts and pages to being able to manage anything the user can think of rather easily. You no longer have to add custom fields to posts — you can add high level support to your own types, creating their own theme page files and admin areas. Since this is a theme based around a business directory, we'll leverage this to create a custom post type to store and display business information.

Designing the Custom Post Type

The first thing we need to do is decide what information we want to store, and the best way to store it.[48] Here is the list of features I came up with:

- Business Name

- Phone Number

- Email Address

- Physical Address (Street, City, State, Zip)

- Website

- Photo

- Description of the Business

- A Category for the Business

Now, we certainly have some overlap between features themselves as well as the capabilities of WordPress. For example, we want

---

[48] I will assume that these are businesses based in the United States.

64 Creating Custom Post Types

to list both the physical address and display a Google Map of the business' location. In this case, we can derive the map from the full physical address, so we don't need a separate field for the map. As far as overlap with WordPress features, by default, WordPress posts include a title, post text area, categories (and custom taxonomies), tags, media uploader, and the ability to designate a featured image within a post. We will make use of all of these, as well as add in our own fields. When we map our features to form fields in the WordPress editor, we get this:

- Business Name ➤ Post Title
- Contact Person ➤ Textbox (custom field)
- Phone Number ➤ Textbox (custom field)
- Fax Number ➤ Textbox (custom field)
- Email Address ➤ Textbox (custom field)
- Physical Address:
    - Street ➤ Textbox (custom field)
    - City ➤ Textbox (custom field)
    - State ➤ Textbox (custom field)
    - Zip ➤ Textbox (custom field)
- Website ➤ Textbox (custom field)
- Photo ➤ Media Uploader ➤ Featured Image
- Description of the Business ➤ Post Text though the main editor
- A Category for the Business ➤ Taxonomy

As you can see, through a combination of stock WordPress features and our own custom fields, we are able to come up with a nice Business Entry page for our theme.

Creating Custom Post Types

65

Building it into the Theme

When working with Custom Post Types (CPTs) we have a couple of options as to how we want to approach them; the two main implementations you might consider are:

1. As part of the current theme (usually through the `functions.php` file).

2. As its own standalone plugin.

There are pros and cons to each. For example, if we're building a CPT that we plan to use in more than one theme, we might want to build it as a plugin, since it will be much easier to move from theme to theme. If we're looking for a CPT that deeply integrates with a theme that we are building, we'd want to build it into the theme itself. Since our CPT is part of our theme, we will be opting for the latter.

Setting up the Custom Post Type

The first thing we need to do is go to our theme and open up the `functions.php` file. We're going to put our custom post type code in a different file (just so it's easier to read/manage), so we'll call that file towards the top of our functions file (I put it at line 31, below the sidebar declaration:

```
require_once('business-manager.php');
```

Now let's actually create the file. Add **business-manager.php** to the *director/* theme. Open it up and add the <?php and ?> tags. The first actual code we're going to add here will define and create our new custom post type.

```
add_action('init', 'business_manager_register');

function business_manager_register() {

    //Arguments to create post type.
    $args = array(
```

66

Creating Custom Post Types

```
'label' => __('Business Manager'),
'singular_label' => __('Business'),
'public' => true,
'show_ui' => true,
'capability_type' => 'post',
'hierarchical' => true,
'has_archive' => true,
'supports' => array('title', 'editor', 'thumbnail'),
'rewrite' => array('slug' => 'businesses', 'with_front'
   => false), );

//Register type and custom taxonomy for type.
register_post_type( 'businesses' , $args );
```

The first line here is a hook in WordPress that will call our function, `business_manager_register()` on initialization. The function itself sets up an array of arguments to send with our custom post type. Most notably, we're setting our admin labels, giving this type all of the capabilities of a standard WordPress post — adding support for the title, editor, and featured image fields, and allowing URL rewrites (for pretty permalinks).

There is one important note about both `rewrite`, and `has_archive`. These arguments are necessary if you want to be able to view an index of your posts without having a specific page template dedicated to it. Using these two arguments, you can now to go *www.your-domain.com/businesses* (or in general, */<post-type-slug>.*)[49]

This function actually has a really extensive list of arguments, giving you a lot of control over the custom post type. Here, I've included what I consider the most important and necessary arguments. You could add many more, such as more of the labels (which can be sent over an as array), the menu position, a custom

---

[49] Actually, there is one more function we'll need to add to make permalinks behave properly. We'll add that in a little bit.

Creating Custom Post Types

67

menu icon, etc. You can read more about all of the arguments for `register_post_type()` on the WordPress Codex.[50]

After setting up the arguments array (`$args`), we pass that along with the custom post type name to the function `register_post_type()`.

The next thing we want to do is register a custom taxonomy for our custom type. This will allow us to add our businesses to categories.

On the next free line of the `business-manager.php` file, add this code:

```
register_taxonomy("business-type", array("businesses"),
    array("hierarchical" => true, "label" => "Business
    Types", "singular_label" => "Business Type", "rewrite"
    => true, "slug" => 'business-type'));
```

This function (which has been part of WordPress since 2.8 — two versions before custom post types!) sends the following information:

- The name of the new taxonomy

- An array of what post types it should be applied to

- An array with:

  - If there can be parent/child categories

  - The menu label for both the plural and singular

  - If we can use this type in `mod_rewrites` (for permalinks)

  - What the category slug should be

As with `register_post_type()`, `register_taxonomy()` has several more arguments we can use to further customize labels and displays. Once again, you can read more about the function on the Codex.[51]

[50] http://codex.wordpress.org/Function_Reference/register_post_type

[51] http://codex.wordpress.org/Function_Reference/register_taxonomy

68   Creating Custom Post Types

Now, we wouldn't have much of a custom type without having some extra info to add to the post. We'll add that info in the form of custom fields. Specifically, we'll be adding several extra fields for the information we outlined above. Since this is quite a bit of code, we'll take it one section at a time. Add the following code to your business-manager.php file:

```php
if (function_exists('add_theme_support')) {
    add_theme_support('post-thumbnails');
    set_post_thumbnail_size( 220, 150 );
    add_image_size('storefront', 620, 270, true);
}

add_action("admin_init", "business_manager_add_meta");

function business_manager_add_meta(){
    add_meta_box("business-meta", "Business Options",
    "business_manager_meta_options", "businesses",
    "normal", "high");
}
```

There are a couple of things going on here. In the first few lines, we're adding thumbnail support, which is necessary to have featured business images. In the subsequent lines, we're telling WordPress what sizes we want our images to be. In `set_post_thumbnail_size()`, we're setting thumbnails site-wide to 220×150.[52] There is a third argument `set_post_thumbnail_size()` will accept, and that is whether or not to crop the image (named `$crop`). We're going with the default, which is false. When `$crop` is set to false, WordPress will proportionally resize the image to our specified dimensions. When `$crop` is set to true, WordPress will do a hard crop, which will not resize the image it all. It will crop it to the proper dimensions.

In the next line, we call another function, `add_image_size()`, which allows us to define new image sizes on top of the ones built

---

[52] Since this is for our own theme, this is OK. I would avoid doing this in plugins since it might cause conflicts with the user's theme. Instead use `add_image_size()`.

Creating Custom Post Types

into WordPress. The ones already built into WordPress, which are reserved words, are: `thumb`, `thumbnail`, `medium`, `large`, and `post-thumbnail`. The Codex strongly advises against messing with these.[53] These words allow us to call a particular image size in our themes, using the template tag `the_post_thumbnail()`, passing the image size name as an argument. So getting back to `add_image_size()`, we want to create a new image size that corresponds to the main image on the `business.html` page in our mock-ups. To do that, we pass the following arguments:

- Name, which in this case is "storefront"

- Width (in pixels), which is 620

- Height (in pixels), which is 270

- Crop, which is set to true

With that, we can freely call `the_post_thumbnail('storefront')` to display a nicely resized image of the business' storefront. There are a couple of important things to note about hard crop: it will resize the image to exact dimensions, so some of your results may be undesirable. However, in this case I felt it was better, so long as we use big enough images. Also, these techniques will not increase the size of the images, which means that if it's smaller that 620×270, it will remain smaller.

After we define the images, we use the WordPress hook `admin_init` to call our function `business_manager_add_meta()` when the WordPress admin is created. That function will add another box to our business type using WordPress's built-in function, `add_meta_box()`.[54] The arguments we pass to `add_meta_box()` are:

---

[53] They say you should **never**. They also say a kitten will die if you do. Don't kill kittens.

[54] The reason we wrap this in our own function is so we can use the `admin_init` hook without completely breaking everything.

70   **Creating Custom Post Types**

- ID, which is given to the new meta box as an HTML attribute. In this case, it's `business-meta`.

- Title of the meta box, which is displayed on the screen. We call ours, "Business Options."

- The callback function that will build the meta box (the fun part!). Ours is called `business_manager_meta_options`. We'll get to that in a minute.

- Post types that this box should be applied to (using the post's slug). For us, it should only be applied to our custom type, which has the slug, "businesses."

- Where on the WordPress editor's screen the box should be (referred to as the context). This is referring to high in the main column (`normal`), low in the main column (`advanced`),[55] or the sidebar (`side`). We've given our meta box a "normal" context.

- Finally, we pass along the priority of the box, which we say is high (options are `high`, `core`, `default`, and `low`).

So as you can see, this function doesn't actually populate the meta box, it just creates it. For populating the box, we look to the callback function we sent as the third argument, `business_manager_meta_options()`. Let's go ahead and add that to our `business-manager.php` file:

```
function business_manager_meta_options(){
  global $post;
  if ( defined('DOING_AUTOSAVE') && DOING_AUTOSAVE )
    return $post_id;

  $custom = get_post_custom($post->ID);
  $address= $custom["address"][0];
  $address_two= $custom["address_two"][0];
  $city= $custom["city"][0];
```

[55] http://wordpress.stackexchange.com/questions/2026/what-is-the-advanced-context-in-add-meta-box

Creating Custom Post Types

71

```php
    $state= $custom["state"][0];
    $zip= $custom["zip"][0];
    $website = $custom["website"][0];
    $phone = $custom["phone"][0];
    $email = $custom["email"][0];
?>

<style type="text/css">
<?php include('business-manager.css'); ?>
</style>

<div class="business_manager_extras">

<?php
    $website= ($website == "") ? "http://" : $website;
?>

    <div><label>Website:</label><input name="website"
       value="<?php echo $website; ?>" /></div>
    <div><label>Phone:</label><input name="phone"
       value="<?php echo $phone; ?>" /></div>
    <div><label>Email:</label><input name="email"
       value="<?php echo $email; ?>" /></div>
    <div><label>Address:</label><input name="address"
       value="<?php echo $address; ?>" /></div>
    <div><label>Address 2:</label><input name="address_two"
       value="<?php echo $address_two; ?>" /></div>
    <div><label>City:</label><input name="city"
       value="<?php echo $city; ?>" /></div>
    <div><label>State:</label><input name="state"
       value="<?php echo $state; ?>" /></div>
    <div><label>Zip:</label><input name="zip"
       value="<?php echo $zip; ?>" /></div>
</div>
<?php
    }
```

It looks like there is a lot going on here, but I assure you it's easy to understand! Let's take it a couple of lines at a time.

72

Creating Custom Post Types

```
global $post;
  if ( defined('DOING_AUTOSAVE') && DOING_AUTOSAVE )
    return $post_id;
```

Here, we are doing two things: grabbing the global **$post** array, which we're going to need to get our custom post values. Then we're doing something **very** important; we're checking to see if WordPress is currently autosaving. If it is, we're going to want to exit out of this function so we don't accidently overwrite anything. We'll do the same thing later on.

```
$custom = get_post_custom($post->ID);
$address = $custom["address"][0];
$address_two = $custom["address_two"][0];
$city = $custom["city"][0];
$state = $custom["state"][0];
$zip = $custom["zip"][0];
$website = $custom["website"][0];
$phone = $custom["phone"][0];
$email = $custom["email"][0];
?>
```

Here is where we get any preexisting values so that the user doesn't have to enter them in every time they want to edit a given post. The function **get_post_custom()** accepts a post ID as an argument and will return a 2D associative array containing all of the post's custom data. We then assign each value its own variable, which will make it easier to manage in the next set of code.

Note: since we can technically have multiple values for each custom post type, that information is also returned as an array, so we need to grab the first value of each array, which is at index 0.

Next up, we define and include a stylesheet that will be used specifically to style our meta box:

```
<style type="text/css">
<?php include('business-manager.css'); ?>
</style>
```

Creating Custom Post Types

73

Come to think of it, we should probably create that stylesheet. Go ahead and add a **business-manager.css** file to the */director/* folder. We'll populate it later.

```
<div class="business_manager_extras">
<?php
    $website= ($website == "") ? "http://" : $website;
?>
```

Now, we start the markup for our meta box. The first thing we do after our wrapper is a check to make sure the website either has a value, or automatically adds the **http://**. Many end users forget to add this information, so it's good to make sure it's there.

```
<div><label>Website:</label><input name="website"
    value="<?php echo $website; ?>" /></div>
<div><label>Phone:</label><input name="phone"
    value="<?php echo $phone; ?>" /></div>
<div><label>Email:</label><input name="email"
    value="<?php echo $email; ?>" /></div>
<div><label>Address:</label><input name="address"
    value="<?php echo $address; ?>" /></div>
<div><label>Address 2:</label><input name="address_two"
    value="<?php echo $address_two; ?>" /></div>
<div><label>City:</label><input name="city"
    value="<?php echo $city; ?>" /></div>
<div><label>State:</label><input name="state"
    value="<?php echo $state; ?>" /></div>
<div><label>Zip:</label><input name="zip"
    value="<?php echo $zip; ?>" /></div>
</div>
<?php
    }
```

Here's the form's markup and the subsequent end of the function. This should look pretty standard, but you might notice two usually important elements missing: the <form> tag and a submit button.

Since we're working within the WordPress editor, we do not need to add either of these explicitly since they are included by WordPress. However, we do need to make sure that WordPress includes them for us. We will do that with our save function. Here's what we have so far:

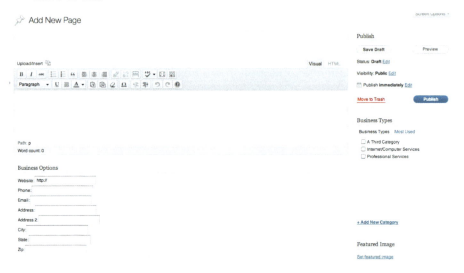

Here are our business options in all of their unstyled glory; let's make them look pretty.[56] Open up `business-manager.css` and add this short bit of CSS code.

```
/**ADMIN STYLES**/
.business_manager_extras div {
    margin: 10px;
}

.business_manager_extras div label {
    width: 100px;
    float: left;
}
```

Not too much here! Truth be told, with these few lines of CSS, we could have added it inline. However, I prefer to separate out the

---

[56] I also went ahead and added some categories.

Creating Custom Post Types

75

CSS, especially of we decide to add more to it later, or call it on other pages.

Much better, don't you think?

So, our meta box looks pretty now, but it doesn't do much. Let's fix that. Here's our save function, which should go right after the display function in **business-manager.php**:

```php
add_action('save_post', 'business_manager_save_extras');

function business_manager_save_extras(){
  global $post;

 if ( defined('DOING_AUTOSAVE') && DOING_AUTOSAVE ){
    //if you remove this the sky will fall on your head.
    return $post_id;
  }else{
    update_post_meta($post->ID, "website",
      $_POST["website"]);
    update_post_meta($post->ID, "city", $_POST["city"]);
    update_post_meta($post->ID, "state", $_POST["state"]);
    update_post_meta($post->ID, "address",
      $_POST["address"]);
    update_post_meta($post->ID, "address_two",
      $_POST["address_two"]);
    update_post_meta($post->ID, "zip", $_POST["zip"]);
    update_post_meta($post->ID, "phone", $_POST["phone"]);
```

```
    update_post_meta($post->ID, "email", $_POST["email"]);
  }
}
```

First, as usual, we have our hook to call our function when the post is saved. In the function itself, we again grab the `$post` array so that we can get the post ID and check to see if the post is autosaving. If we don't include this line, we will lose our data, so it's important we keep that in.[57]

If the post is not updating, we save our custom fields using `update_post_meta()`, sending the post id, the name of the custom field, and the new value. We must do this for every value that we want to save.

This gives us what we need to have a fully functioning Custom Post Type! Go forth and create custom posts! Of course, there are still a few things left to do. Out of necessity, we'll need to create some ways to display those posts. If you look at a business you create right now, WordPress will default to the `single.php` template, making our custom post display like this:

Manifest Development

by **JOE CASABONA** on *Saturday November 05, 2011*
Posted in. |

Welcome to Manifest Development- a one man web development company based in Orange County, NY. Started by Joe Casabona in 2002, Manifest Development's goal is to create a memorable online experience for you and your users through creative design, social media consulting, WordPress development.

/ ARGRAFF DESIGN »

We have the title and description, but nothing else since we use custom fields for the rest of the information. We will fix that, I promise. But first, let's customize our admin panel to display the newly-minted custom information we added.

---

[57] The comment is a homage to Michael Heilemann, who included it in his famous K2 theme for WordPress.

Creating Custom Post Types

Modifying the Businesses Admin Panel

Currently, this is what our admin panel for businesses looks like:

We can improve upon this to display more information. We're going to do two things with two different functions: add new columns to the above page, then populate those columns with information. In the `business-manager.php` file, add this code:

```
add_filter("manage_edit-businesses_columns", "business_
  manager_edit_columns");

function business_manager_edit_columns($columns){
    $columns = array(
      "cb" => "<input type=\"checkbox\" />",
      "title" => "Business Name",
      "description" => "Description",
      "address" => "Address",
      "phone" => "Phone",
      "email" => "Email",
      "website" => "Website",
      "cat" => "Category",
    );
    
    return $columns;
}
```

78

Creating Custom Post Types

When we created our custom post type, WordPress automatically created some new hooks for using the type's slug, which we defined as "businesses." We're using one of those hooks, namely `manage_edit_businesses_columns`, to modify the columns of the admin display. You can find an awesome list of all of WordPress's hooks over at http://adambrown.info/p/wp_hooks/hook. Just replace **{$post_type}** with the slug of your custom post type.

In our callback function, `business_manager_edit_columns()`, we redefine the default array that WordPress uses for the columns, aptly named `$columns`, without our own key => value pairs. The keys are how we'll reference that column, the values are the labels that user sees. Next, we're going to apply some values to those columns. Add this to **business-manager.php**:

```php
add_action("manage_businesses_posts_custom_column",
  "business_manager_custom_columns");

function business_manager_custom_columns($column){
  global $post;
  $custom = get_post_custom();
  switch ($column)
  {

    case "description":
      the_excerpt();
      break;
    case "address":
      $address= $custom["address"][0].'<br/>';
      if($custom["address_two"][0] != "") $address.=
        $custom["address_two"][0].'<br/>';
      $address.= $custom["city"][0].', '.$custom["state"] ▶
        [0].' '.$custom["zip"][0];
      echo $address;
      break;
    case "phone":
      echo $custom["phone"][0];
      break;
```

Creating Custom Post Types

79

```
case "email":
    echo $custom["email"][0];
    break;
case "website":
    echo $custom["website"][0];
    break;
case "cat":
    echo get_the_term_list($post->ID, 'business-type');
    break;
    }
}
```

Using the hook `manage_businesses_posts_custom_column`,[58] we call our callback function `business_manager_custom_columns()`, which accepts a `$column` from WordPress as its argument.

Remember those keys we set up in the previous function? We're going to use a `case/switch` statement to display the proper information in each column.[59] The first thing we do is grab the global post array, and then our custom information. Now we're ready to display the post's information within each column.

Most things should look pretty standard here. If the key matches one of our cases, display that custom information. For the address, we add a little bit or formatting; we also check to see if `address_two` is set. If it's not and we didn't check, we'd have an extra line break.

In the case of the category, we use a WordPress function called `get_the_term_list()`. We are sending the post's ID and the slug of the custom taxonomy we set up, which is all we need to send. We can also send some optional arguments for displaying the taxonomy.[60] In this case, that's not really necessary.

---

[58] The general format is `manage_{$post_type}_posts_custom_column`

[59] WordPress inherently knows how to handle keys like `cb` and `title`. We do not need to define them unless we want to replace them.

[60] http://codex.wordpress.org/Function_Reference/get_the_term_list

80   Creating Custom Post Types

Save your work and refresh your Business Manager page. You should now see something like this:

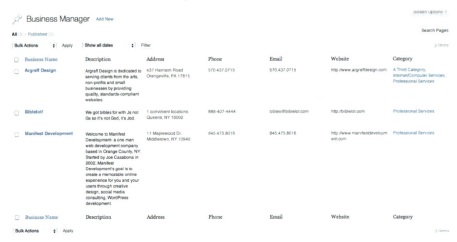

Pretty neat, huh?

Now it's time for the *coup de gras*. Let's modify our theme to properly display our post type.

Listing Custom Post Types

The first thing we want is to list all of the posts that are part of our custom type. Earlier, I mentioned that we need to include two arguments (`rewrite` and `has_archive`) in order to get our posts to display on our site without a specific page template. I also added a footnote saying that's not the whole story. We actually need one more function to force WordPress to apply `rewrite` properly. Add this function in `functions.php`:

```
add_action('init', 'director_rewrite');

function director_rewrite() {
  global $wp_rewrite;
  $wp_rewrite->add_permastruct('typename', 'typename/%year%/%postname%/', true, 1);
```

Creating Custom Post Types

```
    add_rewrite_rule('typename/([0-9]{4})/(.+)/?$',
      'index.php?typename=$matches[2]', 'top');
    $wp_rewrite->flush_rules();
}
```

It's in this function[61] that we specifically tell WordPress that there are other posts besides the default ones, and that we want to include them in the rewrites. We can now view our custom post types by going to *www.your-domain.com/businesses/*.[62]

However, when we go there, we might not like what we see. Since we don't have a default template, WordPress defaults to `index.php`, so we see this:

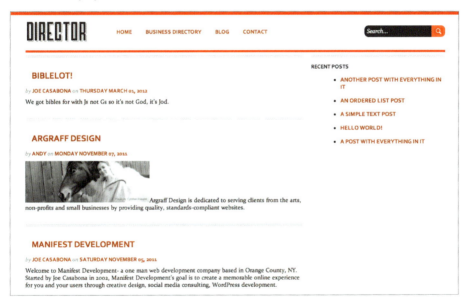

Since we'd prefer something a little more customized, let's create a template that will display our business directory properly. WordPress doesn't accept custom `index.php` pages (something like

---

[61] Thank you, wpAdm: http://wordpress.org/support/topic/custom-post-types-permalinks

[62] Also make sure you have some other Permalink structure besides the default turned on (*Settings* ➤ *Permalinks*).

82

Creating Custom Post Types

`index-businesses.php` won't work), but if we reference the template hierarchy, we'll know that because of the way we configured our custom post type (namely, adding `'has_archive' => true`), we can achieve the same effect by creating `archive-businesses.php`. Go ahead and add the file to the */director/* folder. Now, we'll start the file with the same first few lines that we have in `index.php`:

```php
<?php get_header(); ?>
<div id="main" class="group">
  <div id="directory" class="left-col">

    <?php if (have_posts()) : while (have_posts()) :
      the_post(); ?>
```

The only difference is that while here we have `<div id="directory">`, on `index.php` we have `<div id="blog">`.

Now let's go to the mock-up called `directory.html` and copy what should be in the Loop, like we did earlier with `index.php` and `single.php`. That amounts to the following code, which we will insert right after our Loop definition:

```html
<div class="business group">
  <div class="info">
    <h2>Morbi leo risus, porta ac consectetur</h2>
    <p>Ac, vestibulum at eros. Praesent commodo cursus
      magna, vel scelerisque nisl consectetur et. Maecenas
      faucibus mollis interdum. Lorem ipsum dolor sit
      amet, consectetur adipiscing elit.</p>

    <p class="contact"><a href="#">Site</a> / <a href="#">
      Contact</a></p>
  </div>

  <img src="images/biz.jpg" />

</div>
```

Creating Custom Post Types 83

Now we'll go through and replace all of the static content with information from WordPress, including calling on a function that we saw earlier called `get_post_custom()`. Add this code above what we just added:

```php
<?php
    $custom = get_post_custom($post->ID);
    $website = $custom["website"][0];
    $email = $custom["email"][0];
    $logo = get_the_post_thumbnail($post->ID);
?>
```

For the listing display, we'll only need a few pieces of information that aren't stored by WordPress by default. Anything that we don't see here can be called using WordPress's standard template tags. Aside from grabbing the website and email from the custom array (the same way we did earlier), we're also grabbing the post's thumbnail with `get_the_post_thumbnail()`. This will return the markup for the image, not just the image's URL. The title and description will be replaced by `the_title()` and `the_excerpt()`. Let's take a look at what our info looks like with the replacements:

```html
<div class="business group">
  <div class="info">
    <h2><a href="<?php the_permalink(); ?>"><?php
      the_title(); ?></a></h2>
    <p><?php the_excerpt(); ?></p>
    <p class="contact"><a href="<?php print $website;
      ?>">Site</a> / <a href="mailto:<?php print $email;
      ?>">Contact</a></p>
  </div>
  <?php print $logo; ?>
</div>
```

Much better! This will properly display the business directory info for each business. Now we may want to amend our content section a little bit since if website or email isn't filled out, we'll have dead links. Just change that to this:

```php
<p class="contact">
<?php
  if ($website != "" || $website != "http://"){
    print "<a href=\"$website\">Site</a> / ";
  }

  if($email != ""){
    print "<a href=\"mailto:$email\">Contact</a>";
  }
?>
</p>
```

Perfect. Now the links will only display if there is something to display.

Finally, we're going to finish this template the same exact way that `index.php` ends:

```php
<?php endwhile; else: ?>
<p><?php _e('No posts were found. Sorry!'); ?></p>
<?php endif; ?>

<div class="navi">
  <div class="right">
    <?php previous_posts_link('Previous'); ?> / <?php
      next_posts_link('Next'); ?>
  </div>
</div>

</div>
  <?php get_sidebar(); ?>
</div>
<?php get_footer(); ?>
```

Creating Custom Post Types

85

Now let's save our work and take a look at what we have:

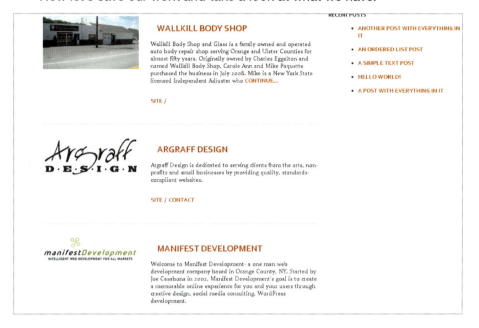

Much better than what we originally had. Now, let's take care of the single post view.

Creating a Custom Post Type Single Template

As mentioned earlier, since we don't have a specific template for our new businesses type, WordPress falls back to the standard `single.php` template; we're going to need more than that. Luckily, WordPress supports `single.php` template customizations via `single-<post-type-slug>.php`. With that in mind, let's create `single-businesses.php`. Add that file to the /director/ folder and add the following:

```
<?php get_header(); ?>
  <?php if (have_posts()) : while (have_posts()) :
    the_post(); ?>
```

If you take a look at the mock-up (`business.html`), you'll see we're breaking a bit from regular layout we've been using up until now;

86

Creating Custom Post Types

namely, we're not using the sidebar. While it's still a 2-column layout, the second column is reserved for the business' contact information.

With that in mind, lets prepare the data that we're going to display on the single post page. Add this to `single-businesses.php`:

```php
<?php
    $custom = get_post_custom($post->ID);
    $contact_name = $custom["contact_name"][0];
    $address = $custom["address"][0];
    $address_two = $custom["address_two"][0];
    $city = $custom["city"][0];
    $state = $custom["state"][0];
    $zip = $custom["zip"][0];
    $website = $custom["website"][0];
    $phone = $custom["phone"][0];
    $email = $custom["email"][0];
    $impact = get_the_post_thumbnail($post->ID, 'storefront');
?>
```

This section is almost identical to what we've seen through the theme, in both the type definition and the `archive-businesses. php` page. The only difference is that with `get_the_post_ thumbnail()`, we're sending a second optional argument, which is used to get a specific size of the featured image. In this case, we're calling the new size we created, which is storefront. The rest, as before, will get pulled from the standard WordPress template tags.

Now, let's look to `business.html` to see what our markup should look line on this page. We'll grab everything in between the `<div id="content" class="group">` and `</div>` tags, which amounts to this:

```html
<div id="business-listing" class="group">
  <div class="info right-col">
    <h3>Contact Details:</h3>
    <h4>The Business</h4>
```

Creating Custom Post Types

87

```html
<p><a href="#">www.business.com</a><br/>
contact@business.com</p>

<p>(123)-867-5309</p>

<address>
    123 Road Street<br/>
    City, State 45678
</address>
</div>

<div class="main left-col">
  <img src="images/impact.jpg" />
  <p>Ac, vestibulum at eros. Praesent commodo cursus
    magna, vel scelerisque nisl consectetur et. Maecenas
    faucibus mollis interdum. Lorem ipsum dolor sit amet,
    consectetur adipiscing elit. Duis mollis, est non
    commodo luctus, nisi erat porttitor ligula, eget
    lacinia odio sem nec elit. Nullam quis risus eget
    urna mollis ornare el eu leo. Nullam id dolor id
    nibh ultricies vehicula ut id elit.</p>

  <p>Ac, vestibulum [...]
</div>
</div>
```

Let's copy this HTML into `single-businesses.php`, but before we start filling it in, we need to treat some of the information to make sure we don't break anything while displaying it. Let's add this next bit of code under our thumbnail call, right before the closing `?>` tag.

```php
if ($website != "" || $website != "http://"){
  $website= "<a href=\"$website\">$website</a>";
}else{
  $website= "";
}

if($email != ""){
  $email= "<a href=\"mailto:$email\">$email</a>";
}
```

88

Creating Custom Post Types

```php
if($website == "" || $email == ""){
    $separator= "";
}else{
    $separator= "<br/>";
}

$address.='<br/>';
if($address_two != "") $address.= $address_two.'<br/>';
$address.= $city.', '.$state.' '.$zip;
```

We're doing a few things here to make sure that we don't produce any broken links and weird spacing. The first involves the website URL. We're simply checking to make sure there is a link and adding the proper markup to it. We have the "else" in the case that website is "http://". Without the `else`, we'd have a rough `http://` on the page. With the email address, if it's not blank, again, apply the proper markup. Finally, we check to see if both website and email are filled in. If they are, we're going to separate them with some marker (in this case, a <br/> tag). We only want that to show up, however, if both are filled in.

What we're doing with the address is essentially the same thing we did on the admin side. If `address_two` is filled out, add it to the full address. Otherwise, just do the street, city, state, and zip.

With our data now displaying properly, let's fill it in with real information, replacing the filler content.

```html
<div id="business-listing" class="group">
<div class="info right-col">
  <h3>Contact Details:</h3>
    <h4><?php the_title(); ?></h4>

    <?php if($separator != "") print "<p>$website
      $separator $email</p>"; ?>
    <?php if($phone != "")  print "<p>$phone</p>"; ?>
    <?php if($address != "")  print "<address>$address
      </address>"; ?>
  </div>
```

Creating Custom Post Types   **89**

```
    <div class="main left-col">
        <?php print $bigImage; ?>
        <?php the_content(); ?>
    </div>
  </div>
```

By now you should be pretty familiar with how this all works. I did wrap a conditional statement around each piece of contact information for the same reason we treated the website, email, and address — to prevent empty or rough tags from showing up.[63]

OK, it's time to close out this template:

```
<div class="navi">
  <div class="right">
     <?php previous_post_link(); ?> / <?php next_post_    ▶
        link(); ?>
  </div>
</div>

<?php endwhile; else: ?>
  <p><?php _e('No posts were found. Sorry!'); ?></p>
<?php endif; ?>

    </div>
  </div>
<?php get_footer(); ?>
```

With this, we add the post navigation, close the Loop, and close the footer. Now, when we visit a single business post, we see this (see top of page 90).

Much better — all of the information we collect is there and now the business pages are distinguishable from the regular blog posts.

There is one more thing we need to do on our theme before moving to option pages, plugins, and resources — the homepage. I've been holding off until we had everything we needed (like actual businesses to display). Now that we have those, let's do it!

---

[63] Notice that I used single line `if` statements, so no braces are needed.

Creating Custom Post Types

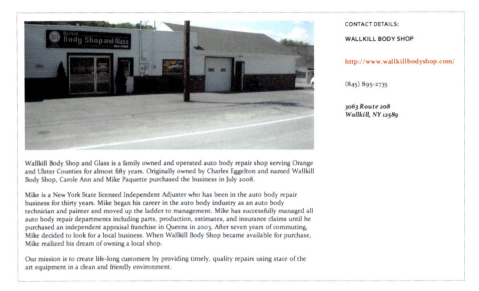

Our single business custom post type in action.

Creating the Homepage

I know it started to get a little repetitious moving towards this point, and some of the stuff we're going to do will continue that trend. But, I'm also going to introduce you to a great friend of WordPress developers, and a way to get new posts.

If we take a look at our mock-ups, we'll see from the `index.php` file that we want our homepage to look like this:

Creating Custom Post Types

91

So, we have some fairly customized elements — a featured business, the most recent blog posts, and the sidebar (maybe even a special one for the homepage only). Let's get started!

First we'll go to the WordPress admin and create a featured businesses category so that our theme knows which business to grab. Go to *Business Manager* ➤ *Business Types* and created a "Featured" category. Keep that title (and slug, 'featured') in mind, as we'll need them in a little bit.

Now let's make our homepage template, which we'll name `front-page.php`. WordPress will automatically make this template the one used for whatever you designate as the theme's homepage in *Settings* ➤ *Reading*.[64] Add it to the */director/* folder and add only the line `<?php get_header(); ?>` to it. While we will be doing various things with the Loop, we'll be building custom queries for it, so let's do that first.

Querying Posts

There are several ways to generate a list of posts to display in your theme. The first (and main) way is to use the function `query_posts()`.[65] This is the main way because this is how WordPress generates the original post or page information when you go to a page. That means that when you use it, you can create your Loop exactly as we've been doing it all along. Consequently, when you use `query_posts()`, it will alter the main Loop information. That means if we do something like this...

```php
<?php the_title(); ?>
<?php query_post($someArguments); ?>
<?php the_title(); ?>
```

... we will get two different titles. Because of this, we want to be mindful of using `query_posts()`, especially when we're generating

---

[64] `index.php` will still be used for the blog posts, as opposed to `home.php`, which will replace `index.php` as the template used for the blog **and** the homepage.

[65] http://codex.wordpress.org/Function_Reference/query_posts

92

Creating Custom Post Types

several different Loops in a single template. A better option (in this case) would be `get_posts()`,[66] which allows us to generate multiple Loops in a single template; the only difference is that we'll have to set up our Loop a little differently. Here is some sample code.[67]

```php
<?php
    $posts= get_posts(array('numberposts' => 4, 'category'
        => 3, orderby => 'title'));

    foreach ($posts as $post) : setup_postdata($post); ?>
        <h3><?php the_title(); ?></h3>
        <?php the_excerpt(); ?>
    <?php endforeach; ?>
?>
```

You'll notice a couple of things regarding the above code. The first is obviously that this isn't the normal Loop setup we've been writing. That's because this line…

```php
<?php if (have_posts()) : while (have_posts()) :
    the_post(); ?>
```

… is reserved for whatever is retrieved from `query_posts()`, which is usually the default information for the page. Instead, `get_posts()` will return an array of posts, which we'll traverse through using a `foreach` loop. To use the regular template tags that we now know and love, we'll call the function `setup_postdata()`, passing to it the current post information (which is now in the variable `$post`). Then, we proceed as normal, using all of the regular template tags.

There is also `WP_Query()`, which is the class used to query posts, create the Loop, and more. While it's worth mentioning here and checking out on the Codex,[68] I won't go into too much depth since

---

[66] http://codex.wordpress.org/Function_Reference/get_posts

[67] I'd recommend checking out both of the above links in the Codex. The argument lists are extensive.

[68] http://codex.wordpress.org/Class_Reference/WP_Query

Creating Custom Post Types

93

we already have a pretty good understanding of the Loop at this point.

Because of the differences and the fact that we'll be calling multiple Loops on our homepage, we'll be using `get_posts()` for both the featured business and the recent blog posts. With that in mind, let's add this code to `front-page.php`:

```php
<?php
$args= array(
    'post_type' => 'businesses',
    'posts_per_page' => 1,
    'tax_query' => array(
      array (
          'taxonomy' => 'business-type',
          'field' => 'slug',
          'terms' => 'featured'
      )
    )
);

$featuredBusiness= get_posts($args);
```

Here we're using `get_posts()` to grab our featured business. If you look at `$args`, you'll see the arguments that we're passing to get our post. This is the breakdown:

- `post_type` – This tells WordPress what kind of posts we want. In our case, we're using the slug from our custom post type.

- `posts_per_page` – This is the number of posts. We're doing one recent post; WordPress will grab the most recent one.

- `tax_query` – This argument accept an array of arrays of custom taxonomies. We'll grab only one with these parameters:

  - `taxonomy` – The slug of the custom taxonomy.

94   **Creating Custom Post Types**

- `field` – Either `slug` or `id`. In this case, we'll be passing the slug of the category we want.

- `terms` – which categories we want. In this case, we only want the featured posts.

We then assign what `get_posts()` returns to `$featuredBusiness`. Now it's time to write our loop. Let's start with the first line:

```
<?php foreach ($featuredBusiness as $post) :
   setup_postdata($post); ?>
```

We have a standard PHP `foreach` loop, and then as I pointed out before, the function `setup_postdata()`. One thing to note is that we have to use `$post` as the variable we pass to `setup_data()`. If we name it anything else, the template tags will not work.

This loop is for the featured business, so let's look at `index.php` for the corresponding code to display out information properly. It looks like this:

```
<div id="featured" class="group">
   <div class="business-info right-col">
     <hr/>
     <h3>Featured Business:</h3>
     <h2>Sem Consectetur Commodo</h2>
     <p>Ac, vestibulum at eros. Praesent commodo cursus
        magna, vel scelerisque nisl consectetur et. Maecenas
        faucibus mollis interdum. Lorem ipsum dolor sit amet,
        consectetur adipiscing elit.</p>

     <p>Praesent commodo cursus magna, vel scelerisque nisl
        consectetur et.</p>

     <p><a href="#">More...</a></p>
   </div>

   <div class="impact-image">
     <img src="images/impact.jpg" />
   </div>
</div>
```

Creating Custom Post Types

95

I think from here, we pretty much know what to do. We'll add in the title, excerpt, a "more" link, and the image that we created. Make the replacements and we'll get this:

```
<div id="featured" class="group">
  <div class="business-info right-col">
    <hr/>
    <h3>Featured Business:</h3>
    <h2><?php the_title(); ?></h2>
    <p><?php the_excerpt(); ?></p>
  </div>

  <div class="impact-image">
    <?php print get_the_post_thumbnail($post->ID,
      'storefront'); ?>
  </div>
</div>
```

We'll finish off the top part of our page by ending the loop:

```
<?php endforeach; ?>
```

One note is that we left out the "more" link. We'll see why in a little bit. Let's do the bottom portion of the page, which includes our blog posts and a sidebar. We'll start with the code before our next loop:

```
<div id="main" class="group">
  <div id="posts" class="left-col">
```

Following this, we'll prepare our next loop. Our call here will be much easier, since we're grabbing the standard blog posts and not limiting them by any kind of custom taxonomy. Add this code, which is the query and start of the loop:

```
<?php
  $posts= get_posts('posts_per_page=3');
  foreach ($posts as $post) : setup_postdata($post);
?>
```

96

Creating Custom Post Types

You can see the only argument we're passing to `get_posts()` this time is the number of posts that we want, which, according to our mock-up, is three. Then, we begin the Loop. What we're putting inside the Loop should look pretty familiar, save for a couple of small differences:

```
<div class="post group">
   <h3><a href="<?php the_permalink(); ?>"><?php
     the_title(); ?></a></h3>
   <div class="byline">by <?php the_author_posts_link(); ?>
     on <a href="<?php the_permalink(); ?>"><?php
       the_time('l F d, Y'); ?></a></div>

   <p><?php the_excerpt(); ?></p>
</div>
```

The only differences between this and what we have on our `index.php` page are that we use an `<h3>` tag instead of `<h2>` for the title of the post, and we use `the_excerpt()` instead of `the_content()`. We made these two changes because if an author forgets to use the `<!--more-->` tag, his or her post will run away with our homepage. There is one small difference in display however: `the_excerpt()` adds an ellipsis (…) to the end of each post.

ANOTHER POST WITH EVERYTHING IN IT
by JOE CASABONA *on* WEDNESDAY SEPTEMBER 17, 2008

Lorem ipsum dolor sit amet, consectetuer adipiscing elit. Curabitur quam augue, vehicula quis, tincidunt vel, varius vitae, nulla. Sed convallis orci. Duis libero orci, pretium a, convallis quis, pellentesque a, dolor. Curabitur vitae nisi non dolor vestibulum consequat. Proin vestibulum. Ut ligula. Nullam sed dolor id odio volutpat pulvinar. Integer a leo. In et eros [...]

Let's take a quick second and change that.

Open up your `functions.php` file and add this code:

```
function director_excerpt_more($more) {
   return ' <a href="'. get_permalink() .'">Continue...</a>';
}
add_filter('excerpt_more', 'director_excerpt_more', 999);
```

Creating Custom Post Types

97

This simple bit of code runs our function `directory_excerpt_more()` when the excerpt is being processed (specifically when the "more" text is being added to it). It simply replaces the original text with whatever we want (which in this case, is a "Continue" link). Save your file and refresh, and you'll see the next excerpt.

> **ANOTHER POST WITH EVERYTHING IN IT**
> *by* JOE CASABONA *on* WEDNESDAY SEPTEMBER 17, 2008
>
> Lorem ipsum dolor sit amet, consectetuer adipiscing elit. Curabitur quam augue, vehicula quis, tincidunt vel, varius vitae, nulla. Sed convallis orci. Duis libero orci, pretium a, convallis quis, pellentesque a, dolor. Curabitur vitae nisi non dolor vestibulum consequat. Proin vestibulum. Ut ligula. Nullam sed dolor id odio volutpat pulvinar. Integer a leo. In et eros CONTINUE...

Much better! You will also notice that the "continue" link was added to our featured business as well. Since this is a site-wide filter, it's added to all instances of `the_excerpt()`. Now, let's get back to our regularly scheduled programming.[69]

After the posts, we have a link to the blog, which we're going to get dynamically. While we could easily hardcode it, we want to be able to use this on any WordPress install, not just ours.[70] Add this code to `front-page.php`:

```php
<?php
  $blogID= get_page_by_path('blog');
  $blogLink= get_page_link($blogID->ID);
?>

<a class="visit" href="<?php print $blogLink; ?>">Visit
  the Blog</a>
```

We're calling a couple of functions here:

- `get_page_by_path()` – This function accepts a page's slug as the argument and returns an object with all of the page's information.

---

[69] See what I did there?

[70] We will, however, make an assumption about the page's slug.

- `get_page_link()` – This function will return a page's permalink based on an ID, which we're able to get through the object returned from `get_page_by_path()`.

Then, it's just a simple print statement. All we have to do now is close out each `<div>`, add the sidebar, and add the footer. We can do that all in four lines:

```
    </div>
    <?php get_sidebar(); ?>
    </div>

  <?php get_footer(); ?>
```

Done! We now have a fantastic homepage that's as dynamic as everything else. There is one issue though. The top orange bar (see here):

This orange bar isn't supposed to be on the homepage. This is another easy fix using WordPress's conditional tags.[71] Conditional tags allow us to check certain things within a WordPress page. We can do anything from checking to see if we're in the admin to checking if the post that we're viewing is part of a specific category. We can even check to see if we're on the front page of our blog, which is what we'll do now. Open up `header.php` and locate line 31, which should simply be `<hr/>`. We're going to replace that with this:

```
    <?php if(!is_front_page()) : ?> <hr/> <?php endif; ?>
```

No we're only printing the `<hr/>` tag if we **aren't** on the front page.[72] Easy and effective! The homepage now looks like this:

[71] http://codex.wordpress.org/Conditional_Tags
[72] Note: depending on your WordPress settings, this **could** be different from the homepage. In our case, it is not.

Creating Custom Post Types

That's it! Our whole front end is now done. Let's start adding some stuff under the hood that will make it easier to manage our theme.

3

Theme Options and Widgets

Creating a Theme Options Page

While we've managed to make most of our content dynamic — that is, we can change it using WordPress's admin panel — we can do even more by creating a theme options page. An options page will allow us to make other areas tied more closely to the templates editable through WordPress's ability to save other values in the database. Specifically, we will make it so, from the admin panel, we can:

- Change the logo

- Insert Google Analytics code

- Add social media buttons to the footer

Sounds fun! The first, modest step is to create a new file named `theme-options.php` and add it to *director/*. Then, we'll include this line in our `functions.php` file (I placed mine right below the line that grabs `business-manager.php`):

```
require_once('theme-options.php');
```

Creating the Admin Page

Now let's open up the `theme-options.php` file and get coding! The first thing we'll do is actually add an options page to the Word-Press admin, under *Themes*. Open up `theme-options.php` and add the following code:

```
<?php
// create custom plugin settings menu
add_action('admin_menu', 'director_create_menu');

function director_create_menu() {

    //create new submenu
```

Theme Options and Widgets

```
add_submenu_page( 'themes.php', 'Director Theme Options',
    'Director Options', 'administrator', __FILE__,
    'wptuts_landing_settings_page');

//call register settings function
add_action( 'admin_init', 'director_register_settings' );
}
```

The first thing we do here is add an action telling WordPress that when the admin menu is created, call our callback function, `director_create_menu()`. In that function, we create a new submenu using `add_submenu_page()`,[73] defining it with the following arguments:

- `themes.php` – The parent page for the submenu.
- **Director Theme Options** – The page title.
- **Director Options** – The menu title
- `administrator` – The capability or level of access for this menu to be displayed. In this case, only side admins can view it.
- `__FILE__` – The menu slug. This is a unique name for the options page. We're simply using the file's name.[74]
- `director_settings_page()` – This is the function that will build the page.

The result is this:

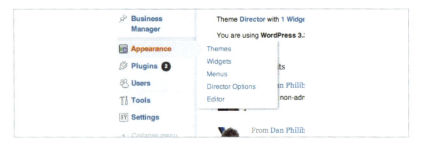

[73] http://codex.wordpress.org/Function_Reference/add_submenu_page
[74] `__FILE__` is one of PHP's magic constants: http://php.net/manual/en/language.constants.predefined.php

Theme Options and Widgets

103

The next thing we'll want to do is actually build the page. However, before we do that, we should register our "settings." That is, we're going to tell WordPress a bunch of variable names that we plan to use in our theme. As you can see, we've added the hook in our previous function, so let's go ahead and add this new function to `theme-options.php`:

```
function director_register_settings() {
    //register our settings
    register_setting( 'director-settings-group', 'director_ ►
        facebook' );
    register_setting( 'director-settings-group', 'director_ ►
        twitter' );
    register_setting( 'director-settings-group', 'director_ ►
        rss' );
    register_setting( 'director-settings-group', 'director_ ►
        logo' );
    register_setting( 'director-settings-group', 'director_ ►
        analytics' );
}
```

This function is pretty cut-and-dry. We create a settings group called director-settings-group and add our settings to it using the function `register_setting()`. This function takes care of how to store the data for us. The first argument is the group name — all of the settings we're adding will be part of the same group. The second argument is the name of the setting. We'll need that for the next step. The function also takes a third argument — a function name for validating and sanitizing data. Since only admins have access to this page, I did not include that function. However, if any other users, or people on the front end, can modify these values, it's incredibly important to sanitize your input data against injections and hacks.[75]

---

[75] To see a fun demo on SQL injections, check out this video: http:// www.youtube. com/watch?v=h-9rHTLHJTY

104 Theme Options and Widgets

We just need to add the mechanism to add values, which we will do in `director_settings_page()`. Speaking of director settings, let's create them. Just so you have an idea of what we're dealing with, here's what the page will look like when we're done:

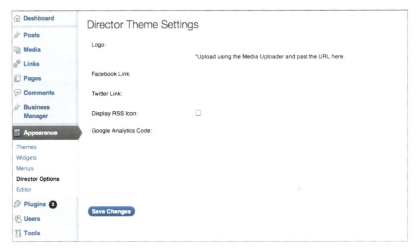

This doesn't look too bad! Here's the entire function, which should go in `theme-options.php`. I'll explain it section by section afterward:

```
function director_settings_page() {
?>

<div class="wrap">
<h2>Director Theme Settings</h2>

<form id="landingOptions" method="post" action=
   "options.php">
  <?php settings_fields( 'director-settings-group' ); ?>
  <table class="form-table">

    <tr valign="top">
    <th scope="row">Logo:</th>
    <td>
```

Theme Options and Widgets

105

```
            <input type="text" name="director_logo" value=
            "<?php print get_option('director_logo'); ?>" />
            <br/>
          *Upload using the Media Uploader and paste the URL
          here.
        </td>
        </tr>

        <tr valign="top">
        <th scope="row">Facebook Link:</th>
        <td>
          <input type="text" name="director_facebook"
            value="<?php print get_option('director_facebook');
            ?>" />
        </td>
        </tr>

        <tr valign="top">
        <th scope="row">Twitter Link:</th>
        <td>
          <input type="text" name="director_twitter" value=
            "<?php print get_option('director_twitter'); ?>" />
        </td>
        </tr>

        <tr>
        <th scope="row">Display RSS Icon:</th>
        <td>
          <input type="checkbox" name="director_rss" <?php
            if(get_option('director_rss') == true){ print
            "checked"; } ?> />
        </td>
        </tr>

        <tr>
        <th scope="row">Google Analytics Code:</th>
        <td>
```

106

Theme Options and Widgets

```
        <textarea name="director_analytics"><?php print
          get_option('director_analytics'); ?></textarea>
      </td>
      </tr>
    </table>

    <p class="submit">
    <input type="submit" class="button-primary" value=    ▶
      "<?php _e('Save Changes') ?>" />
    </p>

  </form>
  </div>
  <?php } ?>
```

So the first thing you'll notice is that this is mostly HTML. Remember, this is the function that is building the theme options page, so there will be a lot of markup.[76] Let's take the first couple of lines of code beyond the function definition and markup:

```
<form id="landingOptions" method="post" action=         ▶
  "options.php">
  <?php settings_fields( 'director-settings-group' ); ?>
```

This code takes us into the form that we use to save our options. At the beginning of this snippet, we name the form and give it the action "options.php," which will automatically handle the form processing for us. We do not need to do any processing ourselves — we're delegating that work to WordPress.[77]

The next line I want to point out is `<?php settings_fields( 'director-settings-group'); ?>`. The function `settings_fields()` is the one that "unpacks" all of the settings that we

---

[76] Normally, I wouldn't use tables either, but WordPress styles them nicely and I wanted to focus on building the actual page. If you want to style the page yourself, you can throw a CSS stylesheet in, the same way we did with `business-manager.php`.

[77] Like a Boss.

Theme Options and Widgets   **107**

created in `director_register_settings()`. That is, we can now
retrieve the values of the settings that we defined in our earlier
function. We will do that using WordPress's built-in function,
`get_option()`.[78] We will pass a setting name to it, and it will return
either its value, or "false" if it doesn't have one. We can also pass
an optional second argument to it; this argument is a string to use
as the default. We will actually see this come into play later. For
now, let's look at the next section, where we build each input box
using our settings. Since this section gets repetitive, I'll take the
entries (one for each type of input) and explain them. First up, the
textbox.

```
<tr valign="top">
  <th scope="row">Logo:</th>
  <td>
    <input type="text" name="director_logo" value="<?php
      print get_option('director_logo'); ?>" /><br/>
    *Upload using the Media Uploader and past the URL here.
  </td>
</tr>
```

For each cell, we create an input box with the name of our setting, and we then use `get_option()` to get the current value. It's
incredibly important that the form element's name matches the
name of the setting, otherwise WordPress will not save the value
properly. Since our form action is `options.php` and we used
`settings_field()`, each of these fields will be processed for us;
no additional coding needed. Pretty neat, huh? Each textbox is
going to work the same way, naming them for each different setting. There are two exceptions though: the Google Analytics code,
which would be better in a `<textarea>`, and the RSS display,
which is just a simple checkbox. Let's look at the `<textarea>` first.

```
<tr>
  <th scope="row">Google Analytics Code:</th>
  <td>
```

---

[78] http://codex.wordpress.org/Function_Reference/get_option

108 Theme Options and Widgets

```
    <textarea name="director_analytics"><?php print
        get_option('director_analytics'); ?></textarea>
  </td>
</tr>
```

As you can see, there isn't a huge difference here; it oper-
ates as a standard HTML `<textarea>`, where we're printing the
value in between the opening `<textarea>` tag and the closing
`</textarea>` tag. Note, again, the input name is the same as the
setting name. After the `textarea`, there is one checkbox, which
is handled slightly differently:

```
<tr>
  <th scope="row">Display RSS Icon:</th>
  <td>
    <input type="checkbox" name="director_rss" <?php
        if(get_option('director_rss') == true){ print
        "checked"; } ?> />
  </td>
</tr>
```

This isn't a huge difference, but it is one worth noting. You can
handle checkboxes as Booleans, which means checked boxes
have the value "true," and unchecked boxes have the value "false."
That is how we're handling our RSS icon option. If it was checked,
WordPress saved it as "true," otherwise WordPress saved it as
"false." We're simply checking the value of it to see whether or not
we should print the attribute "checked." The last thing to do is add
the submit button:

```
<p class="submit">
  <input type="submit" class="button-primary" value=        ▶
    "<?php _e('Save Changes') ?>" />
</p>
</form>
```

Theme Options and Widgets

109

With that code, we've completed a fully functional theme options page. Not too shabby, right? Now, let's add this stuff to the template!

Adding Settings to the Template

Alright — here's the good part! We're going to modify two of our templates: `header.php` and `footer.php`. Let's start with the header. Open up `header.php` and locate this line:

```
<h1><img src="<?php print IMAGES; ?>/logo.png" alt=
  "<?php bloginfo('name'); ?>" /></h1>
```

Right now, it's a static logo that can't be changed without FTP access. We're going to change that. Right above this line, add this code:

```
<?php $logo= get_option('director_logo', IMAGES.'/logo.
  png'); ?>
```

As you can see, we're using `get_option()` to get the value of `director_logo`. If there is no value, we'll use our default logo. The last thing to do is add this to the <h1> instead of what we have now, so that our newly minted <header> looks like this:

```
<header class="group">
<?php $logo= get_option('director_logo', IMAGES.'/logo.
  png'); ?>
  <h1><img src="<?php print $logo; ?>" alt="<?php
    bloginfo('name'); ?>" /></h1>
  <?php get_search_form(); ?>

  <?php wp_nav_menu( array('menu' => 'Main', 'container'
    => 'nav' )); ?>
</header>
```

If we check out our theme in the browser, you'll see that nothing has changed. That's a good sign, as it shows our default value is working since we haven't added a custom logo yet. Let's do that!

Theme Options and Widgets

Use the media uploader to upload a logo and grab the URL. Then paste that URL in the proper box on the theme options page:

Once you save the changes, you should see your new logo!

That's it for the header! Now let's move onto `footer.php`. Open up `footer.php` and add this line of code after `<?php wp_footer(); ?>`:

```
<?php print get_option('director_analytics'); ?>
```

Save your file. Now before we refresh the page to see nothing (notice we didn't add a default value here), let's add our Google Analytics code on the admin side[79] (**Note:** I resized the Google Analytics Code field in my browser to show the entire code snippet.):

---

[79] Really, we can put anything in this box and it will show up in the appropriate spot.

Theme Options and Widgets

111

```
Google Analytics Code:

<script type="text/javascript">

var _gaq = _gaq || [];
_gaq.push(['_setAccount', 'UA-345627-8']);
_gaq.push(['_trackPageview']);

(function() {
  var ga = document.createElement('script'); ga.type = 'text/javascript'; ga.async = true;
  ga.src = ('https:' == document.location.protocol ? 'https://ssl' : 'http://www') + '.google-
analytics.com/ga.js';
  var s = document.getElementsByTagName('script')[0]; s.parentNode.insertBefore(ga, s);
})();

</script>
```

Save Changes

Now if we save our changes and refresh the site (on the front end),
we'll find this if we view the HTML source code:

```
19   <!-- End Footer Information -->
20
21
22
23
24          <script type="text/javascript">
25
26   var _gaq = _gaq || [];
27   _gaq.push(['_setAccount', 'UA-345627-8']);
28   _gaq.push(['_trackPageview']);
29
30   (function() {
31     var ga = document.createElement('script'); ga.type = 'text/javascript'; ga.async = true;
32     ga.src = ('https:' == document.location.protocol ? 'https://ssl' : 'http://www') + '.google-analytics.com/ga.js';
33     var s = document.getElementsByTagName('script')[0]; s.parentNode.insertBefore(ga, s);
34   })();
35
36   </script>
37   </body>
```

Now, onto the last part: our social media icons. Add this code right
after the `<footer>`:

```php
<?php
//social links
  $facebook= get_option('director_facebook');
  $twitter= get_option('director_twitter');
  $rss= get_option('director_rss');
?>

<ul class="social">
  <?php if($facebook): ?><li><a href="<?php print
    $facebook; ?>"><img src="<?=IMAGES?>/facebook.png"
    /></></li><?php endif; ?>
```

Theme Options and Widgets

```
<?php if($twitter): ?><li><a href="<?php print $twitter;
   ?>"><li><img src="<?=IMAGES?>/twitter.png" /></li>
   <?php endif; ?>
<?php if($rss): ?><li><a href="<?php bloginfo('rss');
   ?>"><img src="<?=IMAGES?>/feed.png" /></a></li><?php
   endif; ?>
</ul>
```

There is a little bit more going on here, since displaying the icons are dependent on the values of our settings. The first few lines should look familiar to you: we're simply using `get_option()` once again to get the settings. We then created an unordered list where we display the icons, as long as there is a link to display. Since `get_option()` returns false unless otherwise specified, and PHP handles any non-negative number or string as a "true" value, we can simple use the variables we set up as conditions for `$facebook` and `$twitter`. Since `$rss` is a checkbox, it is explicitly true or false. When all of our social media inputs are filled in and checked off, we get this (with a little help from `master.css`):

With that, we've finished implementing the settings from our options page into our templates.

OptionTree Plugin by Envato

Much like a math class, I showed you the long way only to reveal that there is a shortcut. That shortcut comes in the form of a plugin by Envato, our parent company! The plugin is called OptionTree and you can get it at the WordPress Plugin Directory.[80] OptionTree

[80] http://wordpress.org/extend/plugins/option-tree/

Theme Options and Widgets

gives you a nice area within the WordPress admin interface to create your own theme options without having to code them. You can then add those options to your themes! From the official website: [81]

> **"** With OptionTree you can create as many Theme Options as your project requires and use them how you see fit. When you add an option to the Settings page, it will be available on the Theme Options page for use in your theme. **"**

This can be a great tool, especially if you need to create theme options on the fly, or if you're modifying a ready-made theme. I strongly suggest you check it out!

Next, we're going to create another very popular WordPress theme element: A widget!

Creating Widgets

Widgets are a great way to add secondary content to your website. While you can do a lot with the text widget and generally find a plugin that will give you the widget you're looking for, there is still plenty of opportunity to develop ones specific to your site. In this theme, we're going to develop one to display a featured business right from the sidebar.

Go ahead and open up the `functions.php` file. We'll start by including a file called `director-widgets.php`:

```
<?php require_once('director-widgets.php'); ?>
```

Now let's create that file, and subsequently, our featured business widget. Add **director-widgets.php** to the /director/ folder and add this code:

---

[81] http://wp.envato.com/open-source-plugins/option-tree/

114

Theme Options and Widgets

```php
<?php
class Director_Featured_Widget extends WP_Widget {

    public function __construct() {
    // widget actual processes
    }

    public function form( $instance ) {
    // outputs the options form on admin
    }

    public function update( $new_instance, $old_instance ) {
    // processes widget options to be saved
    }

    public function widget( $args, $instance ) {
    // outputs the content of the widget
    }

}
register_widget( 'Director_Featured_Widget' );
?>
```

This is a slight modification of what we find in the WordPress Codex.[82] Let me explain each function quickly before we get any farther.

First, we have a class called `Director_Featured_Widget` that extends the built-in WordPress class `WP_Widget()`. This class has four functions we can use when building our class:

1. `__construct()` – If you're familiar with object-oriented programming (OOP), you'll know that this is the constructor. This is essentially how we initialize our object. In this case, we will define our widget using the constructor.

2. `form()` – If we are building widget options for the user to customize the widget, we would do that here. We will be using this only to change the title of the widget.

[82] http://codex.wordpress.org/Widgets_API

Theme Options and Widgets

115

3. `update()` – This is how our class would process any form options from the admin panel. Again, we will use this only to change the title of the widget.[83]

4. `widget()` – Here is where all of our magic will happen. This is the function that's used to display our widget to the user.

Alright — now let's fill in the functions we will be using, starting with `__construct()`. All filled in, that function should look like this:

```
public function __construct() {
  parent::__construct(
    'director_featured_business',
    'Featured Business',
    array( 'description' => __( 'Displays the Featured
      Business'))
  );
}
```

What we're doing in our constructor is calling our class's parent's constructor — that is, the constructor defined in `WP_Widget`. This saves us from writing our own function that would do the same exact thing.

We are sending three arguments to the parent constructor:

1. A unique ID for the widget.

2. The title of the widget.

3. An array of other settings. We're only sending the description of the widget (which will show up in the admin).

Next, we have our two interactive functions, which I'll show together:

```
public function update( $new_instance, $old_instance ) {
  $instance = array();
```

---

[83] The code for these functions is a slightly modified version of what's here:
http://codex.wordpress.org/Widgets_API#Example

116

Theme Options and Widgets

```php
    $instance['title'] = strip_tags( $new_instance['title'] );
    return $instance;
}

public function form( $instance ) {
    $title = (isset( $instance[ 'title' ])) ? $instance[
        'title' ] : 'Featured Business';
?>
    <p>
    <label for="<?php echo $this->get_field_id( 'title' );
        ?>"><?php _e( 'Title:' ); ?></label>
    <input class="widefat" id="<?php echo $this->get_field_
        id( 'title' ); ?>" name="<?php echo $this->get_field_
        name( 'title' ); ?>" type="text" value="<?php echo
        esc_attr( $title ); ?>" />
    </p>
<?php
}
```

Even though our functions are in opposite order, I'd like to start with `form()` first. In the first line...

```php
    $title = (isset( $instance[ 'title' ])) ? $instance[
        'title' ] : 'Featured Business';
```

... we have a conditional assignment that will set title to either be the title value defined by the user, or the default value of "Featured Business." `$instance` is the array of values used manipulate our widget.

The next section of the function prints the input box used for the title. You'll see a set of similar functions beginning with `$this -> get_field_`. These are functions that our class inherited from `WP_Widget`. It uses the field name (which gets defined as we call it — that is, if it doesn't exist, create it) as the slug, using it the same way slugs are used throughout WordPress.

Theme Options and Widgets

117

Since there is a singular "save" button that is include on every WordPress widget in the admin, we also have a function within our class to save and sanitize the information. That function is `update()`.

This is a pretty simple function. We're creating a new array for a freshly cleaned set of data. But, since in this case we're only editing one value — title, that's the only value we have to clean. The argument `$new_instance` has the new data from the user, and we use PHP's built-in `strip_tags()`[84] to remove any possibly malicious data. One thing to note is that we **must** match up the keys in `$instance` with the keys in `$new_instance`. If we don't, everything will break.[85]

The fourth and final function that we're filling in is `widget()`, which will display everything to the end user. This is the fun part!

Here's the first half of that function:

```
public function widget( $args, $instance ) {
  extract( $args );
  $title = apply_filters( 'widget_title', $instance[
    'title'] );
  echo $before_widget;
  if ( ! empty( $title ) ) echo $before_title . $title .
    $after_title;
  $args= array(
    'post_type' => 'businesses',
    'posts_per_page' => 1,
    'tax_query' => array(
      array(
        'taxonomy' => 'business-type',
        'field' => 'slug',
        'terms' => 'featured'
```

---

[84] http://php.net/manual/en/function.strip-tags.php

[85] Well, not everything, but our values certainly won't be right.

118

Theme Options and Widgets

```
      )
    )
  );
```

The first four lines of this function handle getting and display-ing the title. The array `$args` contains all of the information related to the widget; this includes any values that we've modi-fied through `form()` and `update()`, and the information we set when registering the sidebar (`$before_widget`, `$after_widget`, etc). After using PHP's built-in `extract()` function[86] to make the key => value pairs in `$args` instance variables, we use WordPress's `apply_filters()` function to prepare our title for displaying on the front end.[87] We then print the markup that goes before the widget (`$before_widget`) as defined in the `functions.php` file, where our sidebar is registered. In the next line, we do the same thing for the title; if it exists, print it wrapped in the markup that should go before and after the title, as defined where the sidebar is registered.

The next assignment should look familiar to you: it is the same exact `$args` array that we have in `front-page.php`. Since we want to grab the featured business for the widget, we want to use the same set of arguments. Then, it's time to display the information in our widget. Here's the second half of our function:

```
$featuredWidget = new WP_Query($args);
while ( $featuredWidget->have_posts() ) :
  $featuredWidget->the_post(); ?>
<div class="widget_featured">
  <div class="thumb"><?php print get_the_post_
    thumbnail($post->ID); ?></div>
  <h3><a href="<?php the_permalink(); ?>"><?php the_
    title(); ?></a></h3>
  <?php the_excerpt(); ?>
</div>
```

---

[86] http://php.net/manual/en/function.extract.php

[87] It will do things like removing slashes and applying any theme-defined filters.

Theme Options and Widgets

119

```php
<?php
  endwhile;

  wp_reset_postdata();
  echo $after_widget;
}
```

You will notice one difference between what we have on `front-page.php` and what we have here; we are using `WP_Query` to grab the post information, not `get_posts()`. Earlier I explained that `WP_Query` was another way to get post information, and it's actually what both `query_posts()` and `get_posts()` use when they are called. The reason we're using `WP_Query` and not `get_posts()` here is because even though `get_posts()` shouldn't conflict with the main Loop, it might; this largely depends on when the widgets are constructed and what information we grab after the widgets are constructed. For example, if we called `the_title()` after our widgets were constructed, might get the title of the featured business, not the title of the page. With `WP_Query`, we create a completely separate object for getting post information, which has its own Loop functions to call. However, the only real change you need to make is that when you reference `have_posts()` and `the_post()`, you need to specify our new object:

```php
while ( $featuredWidget->have_posts() ) :
  $featuredWidget->the_post(); ?>
```

From there on out, it's pretty familiar territory as far as the Loop goes. Once outside the Loop, we called `wp_reset_postdata()`, which will restore control to the main Loop for the page. Basically, it makes sure that our widget info doesn't bleed into the page.

The last thing we do is print the widget's closing markup, defined by `$after_widget`.

Finally, we have to register our widget and close the class. Our final set of code is:

```
    }
    register_widget( 'Director_Featured_Widget' );
    ?>
```

Now when we go to our Widgets page on the admin panel, we'll see our widget:

And on the front end:

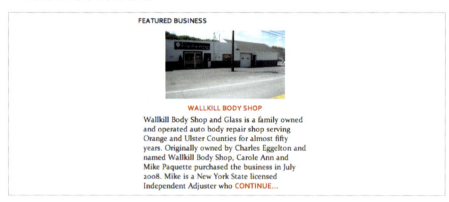

Awesome! We now have a nice little featured business widget that we can display on any sidebar-enabled page.

To complete our project, let's build a plugin!

Plugin Development

Plugins are the heart and soul of WordPress expansion. This is what allows the WordPress community to add functionality to WordPress, expanding it and customizing it to their every need. In this next step, we're going to build a very simple contact form plugin. There are already tons of contact form plugins out there;[88] this is mainly to demonstrate how to develop a plugin. Once you have the basics down, you can go off and develop your own plugin, implementing not just things from this section, but from the entire book.

Defining the Plugin

The first thing we need to do is set up the plugin. Go to the */wp-content/plugins/* directory and create the folder */rockable-contact-form/*, and within it, create a file called `rockable-contact-form.php`. Here, we will add all of the necessary information and code for our plugin, starting with the plugin definition block:

```php
<?php

/*
Plugin Name: Rockable Contact Form
Plugin URI:
Description: A simple plugin that generates a set contact
   form for users to add to their theme
Author:      Joe Casabona
Version:     1.0
Author URI:  http://www.casabona.org
*/
```

This block tells WordPress: a) we have a plugin to include on the Plugins page, and b) the information to display for the plugin. With this information, the corresponding section on the Plugins page is created:

---

[88] http://wordpress.org/extend/plugins/search.php?q=contact+form

124 Plugin Development

☐ **Rockable Contact Form**   A simple plugin that generates a set contact form for users to add to their theme
Activate I Edit I Delete   Version 1.0 I By Joe Casabona

Of course, you could replace my information with your information.

I also like to set up some constants for information I'll be using a lot throughout the plugin. Under the definition block add this info:

```php
define('RCF_PATH', WP_PLUGIN_URL . '/' . plugin_basename(
    dirname(__FILE__) ) . '/' );
define('RCF_NAME', "Rockable Contact Form");
define ("RCF_VERSION", "1.0");
define ("RCF_SLUG", 'rcf-contact-form');
```

I create several constants: the plugin's path, the plugin's name, and the plugin's version, which is used for upgrades, and to notify the WordPress Plugin Directory of changes. Notice that I start all of my constants with "RCF." I'll do the same thing for function names so that we don't create a conflict with other plugins or the WordPress core. Now let's actually write the function that will create the form.

In this section we're going to create the HTML form + code to process it. Add this to `rockable-contact-form.php`:

```php
function rcf_build_form($sendTo, $subject){

  if(isset($_POST['rcf-submit'])){
    include('rockable-process-form.php');
    $rcfProcessor= new RockableProcessForm($sendTo);
    $message= $rcfProcessor->email($subject, $rcfProcessor ▶
      ->buildMsg($_POST), $_POST['rcf-email']);
    print "<h3>$message</h3>";
  }

  $form= '<div class="<?php print RCF_SLUG; ?>">
    <form name="<?php print RCF_SLUG; ?>" method="POST">
      <div>
        <label for="rcf-name">Name:</label><br/>
```

Plugin Development

125

```
            <input type="text" name="rcf-name" required=
            "required" placeholder="ex John Smith" />
        </div>
        <div>
          <label for="rcf-email">Email:</label><br/> <input
              type="email" name="rfc-email" required="required"
              placeholder="ex joe@example.com" />
        </div>
        <div>
          <label for="rcf-message">Message:</label><br/>
              <textarea name="rcf-message" required=
              "required"></textarea>
        </div>
        <div>
            <input type="submit" name="rcf-submit" value=
            "Submit" />
        </div>
      </form>
    </div>';

    return $form;
  }
```

In the first few lines, we check to see if the form is filled out; if it is, we're going to process it. We call a file called `rockable-process-form.php`, which contains a class that I built to process form. Since this class includes no WordPress-related code, I won't go over it here, but I commented it very well using PHPDoc style comments.[89] Just know that it accepts an array of data (usually the $_POST or $_GET array), and emails the results to a specified email address.

You will see our function, `rcf_build_form()`, accepts two arguments: $sendTo, which will be the email address we're sending the form to, and $subject, which will serve as the subject of the email.

---

[89] http://www.phpdoc.org/

126

Plugin Development

The first block of code in the function is what processes the form. If the submit button was pressed, it will include my form processing class, initialize a `RockableProcessForm` object (sending to it the $sendTo email address), and then process the form.

The class's `email()` function accepts four arguments:

1. `$subject` is the subject of the email.

2. `$message` is the body of the email.

3. `$from` is the from address for the email. It defaults to null.

4. `$msg` is the message to display to the user. It defaults to "Thanks! Your message has been sent."

You will see for the `$message` argument, we pass another function from the class called `buildMsg()`. This simply rips apart the data array (in this case, `$_POST`) and emails the information, using the keys as labels and the values as, well, values.

The second part of the function actually builds the form, storing it into a variable that is returned. This is pretty standard, but I will point out that we append a prefix to each input variable name. This is, again, so that our programming doesn't conflict with Word-Press's. Specifically, `name` and `email` are reserved for comments in WordPress, and the page completely breaks if we name our form fields by those names. The fact that the form is stored and returned is very important; if we just printed it, the form would display above all of the content, which the user may not want.

This is our form! You will notice I don't include any validation using JavaScript. Again, this is simple example. If you'd like to include it, you could always use `wp_enqueue_script()`, which I mentioned earlier, during theme development.

Now that we have a way to display it, let's add in a shortcode and a template tag. The shortcode will allow users to insert the slider into any page or post. The template tag will allow theme developers to insert the slider right into their theme files instead. As a theme

Plugin Development

127

developer myself, I think it's incredibly important to include both, and to make them easy to find in documentation. You never know who'll be using your plugin.

The Shortcode

Add this code after the `rcf_build_form()` function:

```
function rcf_insert_form($atts, $content=null){
  extract(shortcode_atts( array('sendto' => get_bloginfo(
    'admin_email'), 'subject' => 'Contact Form from '.
    get_bloginfo('name')), $atts));
  $form = rcf_build_form($sendto, $subject);
  return $form;
}
```

```
add_shortcode('rcf_form', 'rcf_insert_form');
```

There are a couple of things going on here. The last line that we've added here is the built-in WordPress function **add_shortcode()**,[90] which accepts two arguments. The first is **$tag**, which is what will serve as the shortcode. This means we can now type "[rcf_form]" into our WordPress editor and that will be replaced with whatever the callback function, which is the second argument, does.

Our shortcode callback function accepts two arguments as well: **$atts** and **$content**, which is set by default to null. **$atts** is a list of attributes we can send with the shortcode. For example: "[rcf_form foo=bar]". In this case, **foo** is the attribute and **bar** is the value. The attributes are sent as an associative array.

The second argument, **$content**, is any content in between the opening and closing tag, which WordPress automatically looks for. So, for example, in "[rcf_form]Yeah Buddy![/rcf_form]", the content would be, "Yeah Buddy!" We will not be making use of the **$content** argument in our example. We do, however, want to look for a couple of attributes.

[90] http://codex.wordpress.org/Function_Reference/add_shortcode

The first line of our function is a clever bit of code that both sets up the attributes array, and unpacks it into a set of instance variables. The built-in WordPress function `shortcode_atts()`[91] creates an array of attributes to look for, as well as a set of default values. The PHP function `extract()` creates variables out of the key=>value pairs. So in our code, we have two attributes to look for — `$sendto` and `$subject`. Anything else added by the user will not be used. Our default values are the admin email address (as defined in WordPress) and "Contact Form from <blogname>" respectively. Again, these are used only if the user does not define his or her own values in the shortcode.

We then call `rcf_build_form()`, passing our attributes as arguments to the function we created. Finally, we take the returned information, which is the form, and we send it to the WordPress editor. Here's an example of what we could have in the WordPress editor:

In our shortcode, we define a "sendto" address, but no subject. That means the subject will default to what we defined in our function. Here's what we see on the front end:

---

[91] http://codex.wordpress.org/Function_Reference/shortcode_atts

Plugin Development

129

Contact Us

Vitae tortor voluptatem, in fringilla neque. Cursus lobortis habitasse luctus congue nonummy, sodales ultricies rutrum diam, montes lorem sed ultricies convallis nulla, interdum integer in purus, feugiat donec aliquam. Imperdiet aliquam justo lacus, vehicula blandit orci adipiscing dignissim elit, amet vitae, curabitur taciti enim.

Name:

> ex John Smith

Email:

> ex joe@example.com

Message:

>

Submit

FEATURED BUSINESS

WALLKILL BODY SHOP

Wallkill Body Shop and Glass is a family owned and operated auto body repair shop serving Orange and Ulster Counties for almost fifty years. Originally owned by Charles Eggelton and named Wallkill Body Shop, Carole Ann and Mike Paquette purchased the business in July 2008. Mike is a New York State licensed Independent Adjuster who CONTINUE...

… and here is what we see after the form is filled out:

Contact Us

Thanks! Your message has been sent.

Vitae tortor voluptatem, in fringilla neque. Cursus lobortis habitasse luctus congue nonummy, sodales ultricies rutrum diam, montes lorem sed ultricies convallis nulla, interdum integer in purus, feugiat donec aliquam. Imperdiet aliquam justo lacus, vehicula blandit orci adipiscing dignissim elit, amet vitae, curabitur taciti enim.

Name:

> ex John Smith

Email:

> ex joe@example.com

Message:

>

Submit

FEATURED BUSINESS

WALLKILL BODY SHOP

Wallkill Body Shop and Glass is a family owned and operated auto body repair shop serving Orange and Ulster Counties for almost fifty years. Originally owned by Charles Eggelton and named Wallkill Body Shop, Carole Ann and Mike Paquette purchased the business in July 2008. Mike is a New York State licensed Independent Adjuster who CONTINUE...

And there you have it! A fully-functioning shortcode. We can achieve the same exact thing using a template tag.

The Template Tag

Add this code after our shortcode function:

```
function rcf_get_form($sendto="", $subject=""){
  $sendto= ($sendto == "") ? get_bloginfo('admin_email') :
    $sendto;
  $subject= ($subject == "") ? 'Contact Form from'.
    get_bloginfo('name') : $subject;

  print rcf_build_form($sendto, $subject);
}
```

This function is a little shorter, but very similar to what we have in the shortcode. The only real difference is that since we don't have any attributes to accept, we need to assign default values for `$sendto` and `$subject` ourselves. We do this on the first two lines of the function. The third line prints out our form, calling `rcf_build_form()`. If we were to insert this into our template, we might add code like this:

```
<!--Our Loop would be here-->

if(function_exists('rcf_get_form')){
  rcf_get_form('jcasabona@gmail.com', 'Contact Form Using
    Template Tag!');
}
```

This code first checks to see if the function exists (that is, we have the plugin enabled), then calls the template tag using the values that we want. The results would be the same as what we saw with the template tag.

There you have it! A very simple plugin for printing a contact form. Keep in mind that everything we did for the theme (custom post types, options page, etc.) can also be done with a plugin, using the same exact hooks and filters. If you want to add a theme options page for this plugin, just do it the same way we did for our theme. Cool huh?

5

Resources

There are tons of resources out there for developers, designers, and casual WordPress users. As you know from this book, I rely heavily on the WordPress Codex when I'm trying to find new functions, check on current abilities, and see what's coming down the pike. But there is so much more to the world of WordPress than just that.

Theme & Plugin Directories

Theme and plugin directories are a staple for any WordPress user. Whether you need to get a site up quickly and easily, or you need to add functionality to a site without too much development, these directories will help you out.

WordPress Theme Directory (http://wordpress.org/extend/themes/**)**

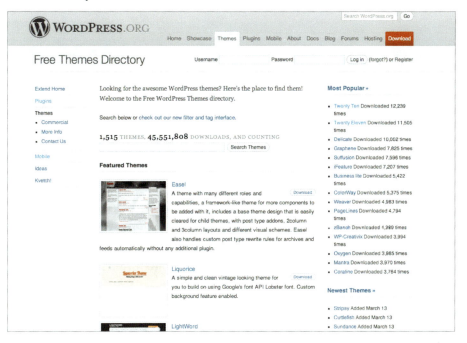

This is the official theme directory of WordPress, containing 1,515 themes, all for free and organized by by title, description, author, and even tag. If you're looking for a free, easy-to-use theme without all the bells and whistles, this is a great place to look. It's usually the first place I go when I'm setting up a quick website for someone. This directory is also integrated into WordPress; that is, you can download themes from within the WordPress admin area.

Themeforest (http://themeforest.net/category/wordpress?ref =rockable**)**

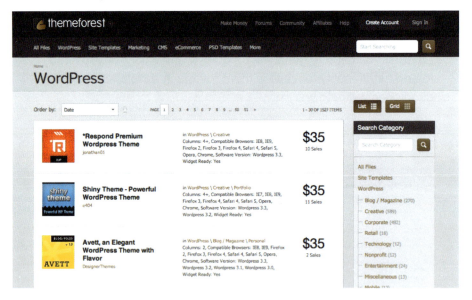

If you're looking for something a bit more upscale than the free WordPress Themes, Envato's very own Themeforest marketplace is a great place to find premium WordPress themes. These themes (ranging from $14-60, USD) are of great design and functionality, including tightly-integrated theme options, post types, and even plugins. Properly vetted by a team of reviewers, there isn't much you need to do to have a fully functioning, custom website up and running in no time.

Resources

135

Elegant Themes (http://www.elegantthemes.com/gallery/**)**

Elegant Themes is another resource I like to use when looking for ready-made themes. For $39/year, you get unlimited access to all of the themes on the site. While their themes aren't as feature-rich as what Themeforest has to offer, you can pick up some really nice themes at a great price.

The WordPress Plugin Directory (http://wordpress.org/extend/plugins/**)**

In my opinion, this is the de facto place to get plugins for WordPress. With close to 19,000 in the directory, all for free, it's likely that you'll find what you're looking for. Plus, just like the Themes Directory, the Plugin Directory is tightly integrated with WordPress so you just search and install.

Resources

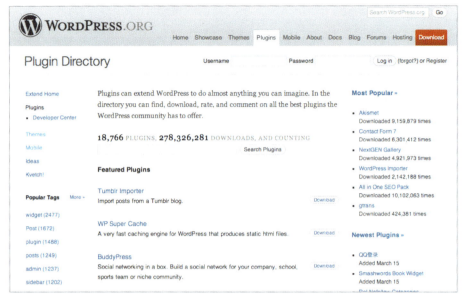

The WordPress Plugin Directory.

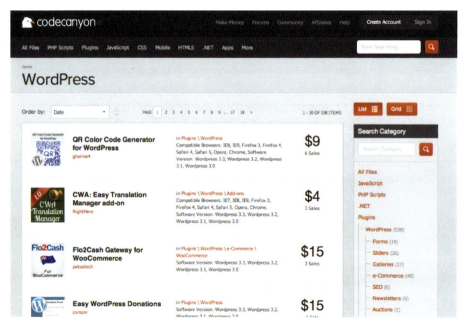

Envato's Codecanyon.

Resources **137**

Codecanyon (http://codecanyon.net/category/plugins/ wordpress?ref=rockable**)**

If you do need something that's not offered in the Plugin Directory, or maybe something that packs more of a punch, Envato also offers a marketplace for code snippets called Codecanyon. They have an entire area of the site dedicated to premium WordPress plugins that are also supported pretty well by the plugin authors.

Coding Resources

On top of resources for you to download themes and plugins, there are books and websites that will teach you how to code specifically for WordPress.

WordPress Codex (http://codex.wordpress.org/**)**

The WordPress Codex is the best source for learning about the WordPress API. Throughout the book, I've referenced it quite a bit to direct you to specific function pages and documentation sections. The fine people at WordPress as well as the WordPress community have done a fine job of keeping this up-to-date and accurate.

Resources by Envato

Envato has a bunch of resources to equip the WordPress developer with everything he or she needs to learn more about WordPress.

- **Nettuts+:** In general, their Tuts+ Network is a great place to learn. With tutorials, news, polls, and more, you'll get everything you need to become a master of your craft. Nettuts+ is directed specifically at web developers, teaching you to use HTML, CSS, JavaScript/jQuery, PHP, MySQL, and more. This is an amazing resource if you're looking to learn more about developing websites. Link: http://net.tutsplus.com/

138

Resources

- **Wptuts+:** Wptuts+ is the part of the Tuts+ Network dedicated strictly to WordPress. You'll learn how to develop themes, plugins, and much more. It's home to a lot of great WordPress specific tutorials (including a few by yours truly). Link: http://wp.tutsplus.com/

- **Books:** Aside from this book, Envato has published two other WordPress related books: *Rockstar WordPress Designer* and *Rockstar WordPress Designer 2*, which take you through the process of designing a WordPress theme, much like I did here.

WordPress Books & Sites

There are also a ton of other WordPress books and websites that have gotten me through the learning process and to the point that I'm at today. Here are a few I would strongly recommend:

- **The WordPress Bible:** This book covers everything I mention here and much more. With 744 pages, it will take you though both using and developing for WordPress, increasing SEO, and marketing your site, all from within WordPress. This should be on every WordPress developer's bookshelf. Link: http://www.amazon.com/WordPress-Bible-Aaron-Brazell/dp/0470937815/ref=sr_1_9?s=books&ie=UTF8&qid=1331831178&sr=1-9

- **Professional WordPress Plugin Development:** This is a book I was reading at the time of writing this, and it's great. It gives you code examples, best practices, and takes you through developing several different types of plugins. This is a great guide if you want to develop market-ready plugins. Link: http://www.amazon.com/Professional-WordPress-Plugin-Development-Williams/dp/0470916222/ref=pd_sim_b_5

- **WPEngineer.com:** This blog is a WordPress tutorial site that does some very cool and advanced stuff. The authors of the

Resources **139**

site have a very deep understanding of WordPress, and they really know how to make it work for them. It's great that they share their knowledge. I strongly recommend checking it out! Link: http://wpengineer.com/

- **Smashing Magazine:** Smashing Mag is a great site for all things related to web development, and they have a site dedicated strictly to WordPress. Their goal is to show some more advanced things and always give the readers something new to look forward to. Their WordPress stuff, just like the rest of their stuff, is top-notch. Link: http://wp.smashingmagazine.com/

Of course, these aren't the only resources out there — there are hundreds more. These are just the ones I use regularly and can recommend to you.

Final Thoughts

Wow! We did a lot here. I covered all of the major bases for developing your own self-sufficient WordPress theme:

- General Theme Development, including The Loop, page templates, sidebars, and more.

- Custom Post Type Development

- Theme Options

- Widget Development

- Plugin Development

I also gave you some great resources to find more information about WordPress development. The number one thing you need to remember is that the Codex is your friend.

With this book, you'll also find the PSDs, HTML files, and theme files for everything we've done here. I urge you to reference and review the files and use them as a guide for future development.

140 Resources

Stay Up to Date!

My last piece of advice to you is to stay up to date with WordPress. You can do so with two very helpful resources:

- **The WordPress Blog:** This site will give you the latest news, events, and updates surrounding WordPress. http://wordpress.org/news/

- **The WordPress Roadmap:** Here you'll get a glimpse of upcoming release and get a better idea of the features and release dates. WordPress releases a major update every 3-4 months so make sure you stay on top of them, as it usually means new features and tighter security! http://wordpress.org/about/roadmap/

About The Author

Joe Casabona is a web developer, writer, and teacher. He hails from Middletown, NY and has been making websites since 2002. His good friend Stephen Mekosh introduced him to WordPress in 2004 and he's been working with it ever since. Joe also writes for WordPress Tuts+ and the Appstorm network. Check him out at casabona.org or on Twitter at @jcasabona.

Since Joe is a big nerd, he'll leave you with one of his favorite Star Wars quotes:

❝ *You fail because you do not see the possibility of success.* ❞ —Obi Wan Kenobi

Your Download Links

Use the link below to download your Photoshop and WordPress theme files for the Director design and theme.

http://rockable-extras.s3.amazonaws.com/wordpress-from-scratch.zip

Printed in Great Britain
by Amazon.co.uk, Ltd.,
Marston Gate.